THE SECRET AGENT

AND OTHER SPY KIDS

10 TRUE TALES

THE SECRET AGENT

AND OTHER SPY KIDS

By Allan Zullo

SCHOLASTIC INC.

No part of this publication may be reproduced or stored in a retrieval system, or transmitted in any form or by any means, electronic, mechanical, photocopying, recording, or otherwise, without written permission of the publisher. For information regarding permission, write to Scholastic Inc., Attention: Permissions Department, 557 Broadway, New York, NY 10012.

ISBN 978-0-545-81814-8

12 11 10 9 8 7 6 5 4 3 2 1   15 16 17 18 19 20/0

Printed in the U.S.A.   40
This edition first printing, July 2015

To Sami, Max, and Joey Manausa, kids with the spunk it takes to be great at whatever they want to be when they grow up. — A.Z.

Contents

THE SECRET AGENT

AND OTHER SPY KIDS

Living
A Lie

Throughout American history, spies have sneaked behind enemy lines, adopted fake identities, and unearthed enemy secrets. They have sent coded messages, worn clever disguises, and used inventive hideaways. Ever since General George Washington created the country's first spy ring during the Revolutionary War, agents have gone undercover in every major national conflict. Their intelligence — information gained by spying — has helped win battles and changed the course of war.

Often armed with little more than their courage and cunning, spies have come from all walks of life — businesspeople, farmers, actors, housewives, doctors, storeowners, and everyday workers. And even kids.

This book features ten stories about the thrilling and dangerous adventures of real-life teenagers who left their mark in the shadowy world of espionage. These young spies chose to live a lie and risk everything — including his or her life — for the good of their country.

The stories — which are based on interviews, diaries, news accounts, and personal journals — use real names, dates, and places, although the dialogue has been recreated. In the following pages, you will read about spy kids from the American Revolution, the Texas War of Independence, the Civil War, World War I, World War II, and the Korean War.

Although each conflict had its own enemy, these young spies all shared a common trait — a passionate belief in a cause that helped shape America.

— *Allan Zullo*

The Carolina Heroine

EMILY GEIGER, COLONIST SPY
REVOLUTIONARY WAR

1781

Sixteen-year-old Emily Geiger shared her father's support of the colonies' struggle for independence from the British. Both wanted to take up arms against the redcoats, but they couldn't for different reasons. Her father John was disabled by a stroke that partially paralyzed his right arm and leg. Emily wasn't able to enlist because girls weren't allowed to join the Continental Army.

"If only I were a man," huffed Emily. "Then I could fight for my country."

"Now, now, dear," said John. "There are other ways to help the cause, like supplying the patriots with our crops."

Emily wanted to do more than assist her father on their sprawling farm located about fifty miles north of Columbia, South Carolina. The Geigers lived among several well-off colonists who remained loyal subjects to the British crown.

Such people were known as Tories or Loyalists. Although the neighbors knew that John Geiger was a Whig — a supporter of the rebellious patriots — he was well respected. As for Emily, they considered her a thoughtful, hardworking girl.

But she was more than that. Having been reared on the frontier, Emily was strong, daring, self-reliant, and accustomed to riding long distances alone.

And she turned into a spy.

Dressed in her blue bonnet and cotton cloak, the lanky brunette would visit Tory neighbors, often bearing a basket of fresh flowers, for a friendly chat. Occasionally, she would overhear conversations of Tories who had returned from British encampments. Sometimes during her visits, her neighbors introduced her to British officers who were passing through. She paid close attention to every detail and then rode off to a rebel outpost and repeated everything she had heard.

But the Tories learned not to trust Emily. She gave herself away because she found it hard to muffle her true feelings. She displayed three traits that no good spy should have: She couldn't lie, she blushed easily when she didn't want to answer a question, and she had a sharp, sarcastic tongue.

One afternoon, she brought over a bouquet of yellow and white, pleasant-smelling chamomile. A visiting British officer asked her, "What do you call them?"

"They're rebel flowers," she replied.

"Why are they named that?"

"Because," Emily said tartly, "they thrive most when they're trampled on."

He understood the double meaning. After that, Loyalist

neighbors clammed up whenever Emily came to visit, although they remained polite to her. She was frustrated because she figured her spying days were over. But she soon got another chance.

In June 1781, Robert Riley, a fellow Whig, stopped by the Geigers' home. He had just come from the camp of General Nathanael Greene's rebel troops a few miles away. Riley told the Geigers that British forces led by Lord Francis Rawdon were marching south toward Charleston. General Greene wanted to attack Rawdon's men, but he knew he couldn't win without the help of General Thomas Sumter's forces, which were about a hundred miles away.

"Greene needs to get a message to Sumter to join up with him," said Riley. "But it's too dangerous because the area is full of bloodthirsty Tories, who most certainly will murder any man who undertakes this journey."

"If only I were a man," said Emily, repeating a wish she had uttered in frustration countless times before.

"Yes, dear," said Geiger. "But you are a young girl — and a fine, spirited one at that."

Why should it matter if the spy who carries the message is a male or a female? Emily asked herself. *I'm just as clever and brave as any boy — and apparently more patriotic. Why don't I volunteer for that mission?*

So, without telling her father, Emily rode her horse to General Greene's camp. She took off her bonnet, curtsied respectfully, and introduced herself. "General, I've heard you need someone to carry a dispatch to General Sumter."

"Yes, but it's an extremely dangerous mission through areas swarming with Tories. It will take the better part of three days."

"Send me," she said.

"Send *you*?" exclaimed the general, taken by surprise. "But you're a young girl! I could not do that. This is a mission that even my bravest men are afraid to attempt."

"I am not a brave man," said Emily. "But I am a brave woman. Just give me a fleet horse, and I will get your message to General Sumter. And I'll spy along the way."

The general was struck by the intensity of her blue-gray eyes and the confidence she displayed. "Hmmm, the Tories wouldn't suspect a girl as a spy. Tell me, Miss Geiger, do you have your father's consent?"

"He knows nothing about my coming here. He loves his country and if he weren't crippled, he would volunteer for this mission. General, my father's heart will say, 'She must not go' but if he let his mind rule, he would agree I have the best chance to succeed. All I need from you is your best horse and directions."

He stared at Emily, looking for any signs that she might waver from her bold statements. Finally, he turned to his aide and said, "Order a swift, but well-trained horse to be saddled immediately."

Greene wrote a note for Sumter and then had Emily read it out loud several times until she had memorized it. That way, if she had to destroy the note, she could deliver the message verbally to Sumter.

At her request, she was given needle and thread. Then she ripped open part of the hem of her petticoat, folded up the dispatch, stuck it in the opening, and sewed up the hem to hide the dispatch. "If I'm detained, it's not likely they'll search me so closely that they'll find it," she told the general. "And now I shall be on my way."

As she hopped onto the horse and galloped off, the general called out, "May heaven and your country reward you!"

About five miles from the Geigers lived Philip Lorie, a Tory. He openly claimed that he was neutral, but through her own spying Emily discovered that he was paid by the British to run a network of spies in the area. What she didn't know was that he had a secret agent in General Greene's encampment.

After Emily had embarked on her mission, the Tory spy went to Lorie and reported, "Greene has found someone to carry his dispatch to Sumter. She left about four hours ago."

"She . . . ?"

"Yes, John Geiger's daughter went to Greene this morning and volunteered. She has the swiftest horse in the camp."

"I knew she favored the rebel cause, but I never thought she was so foolhardy," growled Lorie. "Take my best horse and ride it hard. It will be difficult to overtake her because she has such a big lead on you. You must at least make it to the house of my friend, Bill Mink, a true Tory. He will take up the chase with a fresh horse. Now go!"

Meanwhile, Emily rode through thick forests and skirted swamps, stopping only for short breaks to rest her horse. She took a wide detour around a small settlement that she knew was teeming with Tories, but the route cost her precious time. She had hoped to reach the home of Henry Ellwood, a good friend of her father's, to spend the night, but it was still too far away. It was getting dark, her horse was tired, and so was she.

Clouds had shrouded the moon, and she feared she would lose her way in the darkness if she went much farther. Then she heard a dog bark and spotted a house where a middle-aged couple was sitting on the porch.

After helping her off her horse, the man said, "I'm Ronald Preston and this is my wife, Jane." Pointing to his black Labrador retriever, he added, "That's Raven. And who might you be?"

Emily couldn't think quick enough to come up with a fake name, not that she would have because she simply couldn't lie. Hoping that they had not heard of her father, she replied, "I'm Emily Geiger." She was relieved when the Prestons showed no signs that they recognized the name. "I'm on my way to see my father's friend Henry Ellwood"— she started to blush —"about a personal matter."

"Ellwood's place is about ten miles away," said Mr. Preston. "You best spend the night with us."

Added Mrs. Preston, "It's hardly safe for a young girl like you to take such a journey alone in these troubled times."

"I'm not afraid. No one will harm me," said Emily, forcing a smile as she untied the strings of her bonnet.

"I'm not so certain of that, child," said Mr. Preston. "It's only a few days since Greene and his men passed here in full retreat. No doubt there are many straggling vagabonds from his army roaming around who would make it unsafe for you."

"Those nasty rebels," muttered Mrs. Preston, her voice tinged with scorn.

A chill crept over Emily. *Just my luck,* she thought. *I'm at the home of Tories! If they ask any questions about the war, change the subject. Make them think you're just a naïve farm girl.*

She tried to take control of the conversation during dinner, talking about farming and the weather and the Prestons' lovely home. Although there were no pointed questions, she blushed a lot, and tried to cover up her discomfort by feeding Raven table scraps. After dinner, Emily excused herself and went to bed. Before falling asleep, she heard the Prestons whispering to each other.

"She's John Geiger's daughter," said Mr. Preston. "He's a Whig!"

"Why would she be riding way out here? And in such a hurry?"

"Maybe she's a spy."

"Oh, Ronald, a young girl like her a spy? I don't think the rebels are that desperate. Still, it is cause for wonder. What should we do?"

"Let's think about it. She won't be going anywhere tonight. She's asleep."

They know who I am! thought Emily. *I'll wait until they fall asleep and then I'll sneak out of here.*

But two hours later, she heard a horse rapidly approaching the house. "Hello, Preston!"

"Why, it's Bill Mink!" declared Mr. Preston when he opened the door. "What brings you out here at this time of night?"

"Have you seen anything of a stray young girl in these parts?"

"Yes, I have. Why?"

"I have it on good authority that the daughter of that Whig John Geiger is carrying an important message to General Sumter. She has a head start on me, but I need to catch and detain her and make sure the message doesn't get through. Any idea where she is?"

"Hush, Bill, and come inside."

Emily heard every word from her bed. She got up and pressed her ear against the bedroom door. Although Mink was whispering to the Prestons, she heard him say he planned to let her sleep through the night, then tie her up in the morning, and take her directly to General Rawdon.

As nervous sweat trickled down her arms and legs, Emily remained still for more than an hour until she was sure the three of them were asleep. Ever so quietly, she put on her clothes and tiptoed to the open window. She looked out and saw that the clouds had parted and the moon had risen over the treetops. *At least I won't be riding in total darkness,* she thought. *That's a good break.*

Crawling out of the window, she felt her feet hit the ground a second before something touched the back of her leg. She gasped and her whole body trembled. Holding her breath, she slowly turned to see who had caught her. *Is it Mink? Mr. Preston?* At first glance she saw no one. Then she exhaled and silently giggled when she realized it was the couple's dog, Raven.

Emily petted him, hoping he wouldn't bark and give her away. Seeing his tail wag, she continued to give him attention as he followed her to the stable. *I'm glad I fed him at the table,* she thought. In the blackness, it took longer than expected to find her bridle and saddle and to determine which of the four horses inside was hers. All this had to be done without making a sound or causing the animals to alert Mink or the Prestons.

Once her horse was saddled, she walked it away from the

house. She wanted to hop on her steed and gallop off, but she knew that would awaken Mink and trigger a chase in the dark. So she kept walking, with Raven by her side, all the while praying that no one in the house would get up and realize she had left.

Finally, Emily figured she was far enough away to mount her horse. Raven tagged along for a few hundred yards and then turned back toward the house.

Reaching Ellwood's house just before dawn, Emily confided to him the nature of her mission and her close call with the Prestons and Mink. Ellwood gave her a quick breakfast, a strong horse, directions to the home of a friend — a fellow Whig, about twenty miles away — and a letter of introduction. When she arrived at the next stop, the friend read Ellwood's letter and let Emily take a fresh horse.

Early in the evening, about thirty miles from General Sumter's encampment, Emily was wondering where she would spend the night. As she galloped around a bend, her heart sank. Up ahead were three horsemen dressed in British uniforms. *If I turn and go back, it will raise suspicion*, she thought. *I have to keep going. Maybe they will ignore me and let me go on my way.*

"Good evening, gentlemen," she said.

"Whoa, there, young missy," said the leader. He grabbed the bridle of her horse and then fired questions at her. Who was she? Where was she going? For what purpose? Why was a young girl traveling alone and in such a hurry?

Blushing and evasive, Emily answered the questions in short, clipped responses, none to the satisfaction of the soldiers.

"It seems to me that you might be involved with the rebel cause," said the leader.

11

"And most probably a spy," added one of the soldiers.

There's no escape, she thought. *I must find a way to destroy the dispatch before it's discovered on me. How can I convince them I'm just a farm girl who got lost?*

Holding the reins of her horse, the soldiers took Emily to Lord Rawdon's encampment, which was only about a mile away. She was led into his tent where he asked her the same questions that she had fielded minutes earlier. The vague responses from the blushing girl made the general suspicious.

Frustrated with her answers, he bellowed, "We'll find a way to the truth!" Turning to his aide, he said, "Take her over to my quarters, and see that she doesn't escape."

Under armed guard, Emily was led to a nearby farmhouse and locked alone in a bedroom. *Here's my chance to destroy the dispatch,* she told herself. Not knowing if she had only seconds or minutes, she hurriedly ripped open the hem of her dress and took out Greene's folded message.

I can't throw it out the window. The guards will spot it. Maybe I can rip it up and hide the pieces in here somewhere. A quick glance around the room convinced her it wasn't secure enough to conceal the pieces. *They'll probably bring someone in to search me and every part of this room. I must get rid of it now!*

She wished she could think more clearly, but she was scared and tired and hungry. Her stomach gurgled because she hadn't eaten since dawn. *My stomach! Of course!* She tore off a part of the dispatch, thrust it into her mouth, chewed, and swallowed it. Then she ripped another piece and ate it. It was hard to get down without water but between a few chokes, she managed. Unfortunately, before the last piece was consumed, the door flung open and an older woman, a Loyalist, entered.

Turning her back to the woman, Emily shoved the remaining paper into her mouth. Then she covered her face tightly with her hands and pretended to weep until she had swallowed the last piece of the telltale dispatch.

"Oh, quit your wailing," snapped the woman, "and face me."

Emily turned around and, acting offended, demanded, "By what authority am I made a prisoner in this room?"

"By the authority of Lord Rawdon," the woman answered gruffly.

"I would think a man of his lofty military position would have more important things to do than make a prisoner of a young girl who had the misfortune of getting lost and being rudely confronted by his scouts."

"You'd better keep your saucy tongue still, or it may get you into worse trouble," replied the woman. "You are suspected of being a spy — the bearer of a dispatch from General Greene, and it's my business to find it."

Emily spread out her arms and said, "Go ahead and search. I have nothing to hide."

Very slowly and deliberately, the woman searched Emily. *Hurry up, hurry up,* Emily thought. *I must get out of here before Mink arrives or I will never get the message to Sumter.*

The woman found nothing, except for a tear in the hem of Emily's dress. "And what happened here?" she asked, pointing to the rip.

"A casualty of riding. My hem got caught on a low branch. But how would you know of such things? You probably can't even ride a horse."

The woman stormed out of the room and moments later two guards came in and searched the entire room. When they couldn't find any evidence of a dispatch, General Rawdon apologized to Emily and told her she was free to go.

"I should hope that if your men meet another fair citizen of this colony, she will be treated with more civility and less suspicion," said Emily. Then she rode off, but not before making a mental note of the number of troops she had counted and where they were located. Not wasting another moment, she galloped off and arrived about an hour later at the home of another Whig, George Simpson.

She was just getting ready to eat a quick dinner when Simpson's 18-year-old son, Jacob, rushed into the house. "A horseman stopped me on the road and asked if I had seen a young girl in a blue bonnet. I told him no and he rode off at full speed in the direction of Rawdon's encampment."

"That must be Mink!" declared Emily, leaping to her feet. "I must go instantly! The British will be looking for me within the hour, and if they catch me, they surely won't let me go free."

"But it's so dark outside," said Simpson. "You won't be able to find your way."

"I have no choice. I must get the message to Sumter."

"All right, here's what we'll do," said Simpson. "I'll give you a fresh horse and Jacob will guide you through these woods. He knows them very well. But you will have to take a detour because the British will be looking for you on the road to the Wateree River where Sumter is."

Emily and Jacob rode through the night in the dark without encountering any soldiers. At sunrise, Jacob gave her directions to Sumter's encampment and bid her good luck. Then he headed back home.

Without stopping to refresh either herself or her tired horse, Emily pressed forward, though the summer heat grew increasingly intense as the sun crept higher in the sky. Faint from hunger and thirst and weak from exhaustion, she urged her weary horse to keep going. *How much farther?* she wondered. *Will I ever make it before I pass out or my horse falters? I'm so tired, so . . .*

Emily slumped over until her head lay on the horse's mane. Letting go of her reins, she slipped off her saddle and tumbled to the ground, unconscious.

She was revived when water was splashed on her face. Fluttering her eyes until they focused, she smiled because she was looking up at two soldiers from the Continental Army.

"Please," she mumbled, "take me to General Sumter. It's very important."

"Perhaps you should rest a spell," said one of the soldiers. "You took a nasty spill."

"My horse?"

"He's tied up. We found him a couple hundred yards from here."

Judging from the position of the sun, she figured she had been unconscious for about an hour. *Mink is probably only minutes behind us. If he sees me, he'll shoot me to stop me from delivering the message.*

"We must leave now," she insisted. As she got to her feet, she became dizzy and plopped to the ground.

"You're in no condition," said the soldier.

Gritting her teeth, she said, "Soldier, help me onto my horse and get me to the general right now. We have no time to spare."

The soldiers did what they were told and then rode on each side of her all the way to the camp. When they arrived, they helped her off her horse and into the general's tent. With each step, her body rallied with renewed vigor, and by the time she came face-to-face with Sumter, she clearly blurted out Greene's important message that she had memorized word for word.

Within the hour, Sumter and his men were marching to join with Greene's forces. Days later, the Continental Army clashed with Rawdon's troops in Biggin Church, South Carolina, in a fierce battle that ended with the British in retreat.

It took nearly two weeks before Emily returned safely to her worried father. At their tearful reunion, he told her, "I learned of your mission two hours after you had left. I was worried sick every second of every day, wondering if I would ever see you again."

"I had no doubt that I would see you, Father."

"What a courageous patriot you are — brave, if not braver, than any young man. I am so proud of you. But promise me one thing."

"Anything, Father."

"You are a remarkable young woman and I don't ever want to hear you say, 'If only I were a man.'"

Emily gave up spying, though she and her father continued to supply food to the Continental Army until the British were driven out of South Carolina the following year. The war between Britain and the United States officially ended in 1783. Emily married a plantation owner in 1789 and lived the rest of her life near where she grew up.

The Texas Rat

KIT BENSON, SPY FOR GENERAL SAM HOUSTON
TEXAS WAR OF INDEPENDENCE

1836

The door to the little log cabin burst open and Kit Benson's father, Raymond, shouted, "Gather what you can! We must flee immediately!"

"Is it Santa Anna and his army?" asked Kit.

"Yes. They're marching this way and burning everything in their path. We've got to get out of here right now!"

"Raymond, what's happening?" Kit's mother, Sarah, yelled.

"Those butchers!" Raymond snarled, pounding his clenched hand into his palm. "Word has it that they took the Alamo and killed everyone there. And when the soldiers at Goliad surrendered, they took them out and slaughtered them, too! Santa Anna is burning entire towns. There's little hope now for any of us because General Houston keeps retreating."

The hardscrabble life that Kit and his parents were living since they moved to the Mexican-held territory of Texas had suddenly taken a turn for the worse. Years earlier, they and thousands of other Americans had settled in Texas at the encouragement of the Mexican government. But over time the Mexican President, General Antonio Lopez de Santa Anna, had turned into a ruthless dictator. Outraged by his iron-fisted rule, some Texas settlers revolted and demanded independence. Other Texans like the Bensons who hadn't taken up arms were now caught in the middle of an increasingly violent uprising.

"We have to pack up what we can and head for Galveston," said Raymond. "We will stay with my brother."

"I can't believe this is happening," Sarah sobbed.

As Kit donned his coonskin cap and rushed to throw what few possessions he had in his knapsack, he doubted if they would see their homestead again. Ever since moving here from Alabama three years earlier, the 14-year-old had learned to love the backwood swamps where he would sneak among the palmettos, hunting white-tailed deer, squirrels, and rabbits. For a boy his age — the curly-haired lad looked no older than ten because of his small size — he was a remarkable hunter and an even better fisherman. And that was a good thing because he supplied most of the meat and fish for the family table.

Being uprooted, Kit wondered if he would ever again see his best friend, Luis Delgado, a Mexican-born Texan, who often went fishing with him. The two had taught each other their native languages — or at least enough to get by. They enjoyed competing against each other, especially hitting targets by throwing their knives, shooting their rifles, or flinging rocks. *Are we enemies now?* he asked himself. *If so, maybe it's good that we leave. I don't want to be enemies with Luis just because he's Mexican.*

Kit knew that times were tense. Santa Anna and his huge Mexican force charged into the Texas town of San Antonio to squash the revolt. With a take-no-prisoners ferocity, the army stormed a Spanish mission there called the Alamo — a fortress manned by supporters of independence — and killed all 187 defenders. Then weeks later, Santa Anna's troops surrounded a rebel stronghold at Goliad, promising safe passage to the United States if its 400 rebel soldiers surrendered. The soldiers agreed — only to be herded into an open field and massacred.

Meanwhile, General Sam Houston, commander of the Texas army, fled east with his ragtag force of less than a thousand men, hoping to avoid any major clashes with Santa Anna's experienced soldiers. That is, until the time was right for his rebel army to attack the troops of the overconfident Mexican general.

The Bensons said good-bye to their sturdy hand-built one-room cabin. With their possessions thrown in their rickety horse-drawn cart, they began the trek to Galveston about 75 miles away.

For settlers like the Bensons in southeast Texas, it was a time of terror and frenzy in what was later called the Runaway Scrape. In a mad scramble to escape the advancing, deadly Mexican forces, people left food on their tables, hastily packed their saddlebags, valises, and wagons, and headed east. Rain and cold weather turned roads and trails into thick muddy bogs and swelled streams, slowing the frantic settlers' eastward progress and creating even more panic.

Hearing from others on the refugee trail, Kit grew to believe that Texans deserved their independence from Mexico and its corrupt government and abusive military. But he, like so many others who had abandoned their homes, wondered if they would ever really be free.

Food was scarce on the trail, but thanks to Kit's hunting skills, he and his parents had enough to eat. On the fourth day of their journey, he headed off into the woods in search of prey. The plan was for him to meet up with his parents at a river crossing several miles away. If they didn't connect for whatever reason, they were to continue on their way to Galveston and hope to be reunited there.

As evening approached, a cold, hard rain blew. Needing shelter, Kit was looking for a hollow log or cave when he came across a boarded-up cabin. He knocked but when no one answered, he went inside and saw it had been abandoned in a hurry. Coals in the fireplace were still warm but the place had been stripped of personal possessions, even the furniture. The cabin had a main room and a bedroom and a wooden ladder to an open loft. *I'll wait here until the rain lets up*, he thought.

He put some firewood in the hearth and was about to light it when he heard the whinny of horses and the galloping of hooves. *Would it be my luck that the Mexicans are coming here?* He instinctively reached for his rifle, which was as big as he was. Cocking his ear, he heard the approaching horses and then human voices. They were speaking in Spanish.

His heart began to race. *They're heading for the cabin. But I can't fight them here alone. I'll be killed.* He thought about running off, but he was afraid he would be spotted because with the windows boarded up, the only way out was through the front door. There was only one thing to do — hide in the loft.

As the Mexicans reached the cabin, Kit scrambled up the ladder to the loft, which had a few empty boxes and a large wooden trunk. Carefully, so he wouldn't make any noise, he moved the trunk to create a space between it and the wall so he could hide.

Seconds after he got settled, the door swung open. He heard several voices — he guessed maybe four or five Mexicans. When they lit a fire, the light shot up through the cracks in the floor of the loft. Kit cautiously lay flat on his belly so he could see what was happening below him.

By their blue uniforms, he knew they were officers of the Mexican army. One of them had a very dignified appearance and was addressed with respect. *He must be the leader of this group, like a colonel,* Kit thought. *Thank goodness, Luis taught me Spanish. At least I'll figure out what they're saying.* The leader took a piece of parchment out of his pocket, opened it, and spread it flat on the floor.

Kit's keen eyes saw that it was a crude map of the area with several dots and arrows. Pointing to a spot on the map, the colonel said, "The rebels are here. We can make the march tomorrow around this swamp and surprise General Houston and his rabble early the following morning. Then our work will be over." He tapped the spot of the anticipated ambush and grinned. The others nodded in agreement.

Just then Kit felt something crawling up his leg. It was a rat. Without thinking, he shook his leg, causing a board to creak and a pinch of dust to float down toward the men. In an instant the soldiers below sprang up and looked toward the loft.

"Is someone up there?" the leader shouted. Turning to one of his men, he ordered, "Go check it out."

If they find me, they'll kill me for sure, Kit thought. Ever so carefully he curled up behind the trunk. But then he saw that his rifle was sticking out. *If the light hits the barrel, they'll look behind the trunk.* He took off his coat and threw it over the exposed part of the rifle.

The soldier climbed the ladder until he was eye-level with the floor of the loft. Holding a candle, he peered around the loft. "Nothing here but some boxes and a trunk . . . and a very big rat."

"The only rat I want to kill is named Sam Houston," said the colonel. Then he and his fellow officers turned their attention back to the map.

I've got to warn General Houston, Kit told himself. *But they'll hear me if I try to leave. I need to divert their attention for a few seconds, but how?*

The pesky rat had waddled near him, and Kit had an idea. In his knapsack was a piece of pork saltback. He quietly broke off a piece and placed it by his side. The rat took the bait and when it was close enough, he grabbed it. The rodent made a little squeal, but if the men heard it, they ignored it.

Slowly, Kit straightened up and, while holding the rat in one hand, he grabbed his rifle and slung it over his back. Then he leaned over the open loft and tossed the rat down onto the officers. The startled men jerked away and then, seeing the rat, they laughingly gave chase around the room.

Meanwhile, Kit tossed his knapsack over his shoulder and silently unlatched the shutter of the loft window. He slipped outside and then, even though it was raining, climbed down the logs with the skill of a mountain climber. By now, he could tell that the men had heard noise coming from the loft and were investigating. He dropped the final four feet to the ground.

Making his way to the horses, which were tied up to nearby trees, he approached them with caution so they wouldn't be spooked and alert the officers. The horses stood quietly while he carefully untied the nearest one. His heart pounding, Kit talked soothingly to the horse as he led it away into the darkness. About 100 yards from the cabin, he mounted the steed and took off for Sam Houston's camp. He kept hoping that his memory of what he saw on the map was sharp enough to lead him to the general.

Two hours later, Kit was trotting on his horse, grateful that the rain had stopped, when a man in the rough garb of a frontiersman emerged from the darkness, pointed a rifle at him and barked, "Halt! Who goes there?"

"Is this General Houston's camp?" Kit asked.

"That depends on who you are."

"I'm Kit Benson, and I believe in Texas independence. I was spying on some Mexican officers and I have some important news for General Houston."

"Then you found us, boy. Dismount and follow me."

A few minutes later they entered an encampment lit by a few fires burning low in a secluded valley. The soldiers, bearded and ragged from forty days in the field, were a fierce-looking band. But their long rifles looked clean and well-oiled.

Standing near one of the fires with his back to Kit was a tall, burly man whose large hands were folded behind him as if he was in deep thought. He turned around, revealing deep-set, penetrating eyes that stared out from under heavy brows. Even though the boy had never seen him before, Kit knew he stood in the presence of General Houston, the champion of Texas liberty. Houston, his clothes mud-splattered and frayed, fixed his gaze on Kit and motioned him forward. "Tell your story, son."

The general listened without interruption to every word as Kit relayed what he had seen and heard. When Kit finished, Houston said, "You did well to escape, son, because if you hadn't, I wouldn't have given much for the head that wears your coonskin cap."

"Yes, sir."

The general pulled out a map and with the light of a candle had Kit point out what he saw on the Mexicans' map. "Santa Anna expects us to go south around the swamp, which is what we had planned to do," said Houston. "But we will go north so when he springs his so-called trap, he will catch nothing except maybe a cold." He slapped Kit on the back and said, "You are a good spy, and for a lad of your age, you have the wits of a seasoned soldier."

"I'm glad to be of service to you, General."

Because it was now too dangerous for Kit to travel alone, he chose to stay with Houston's army. He figured that even without him, his parents would have enough food to make it to Galveston. Before daybreak, the men broke camp and headed north, away from Santa Anna's troops and continued along a zigzag path toward Galveston.

During the march, Kit was taken under the wing of a grizzled middle-aged soldier, Private John Coker, of the 2nd Regiment Volunteers Calvary/Spy Company, who, like Kit, had come from Alabama. "My given name is John, but I prefer Jack," he said. "Been in Texas a couple years. I'm a blacksmith by trade, but I'm willin' to fight for independence. Besides, if we win, all us soldiers will be given our own land. Pretty good deal, wouldn't you say?"

"Let me be of help to you," said Kit. "I'm a good shot and a good spy."

Jack took off his soiled, tattered brimmed hat and scratched his bald scalp. "Boy, the best thing you can do is keep our rifles well-oiled . . . and if we're attacked, duck for cover."

"There are some boys close to my age, and they're fighting."

"Why, you can't be older than twelve. Too young."

"I'm fourteen. And I'm a good spy. Even the general himself said so."

Jack laughed. "Okay, then, you can be our unofficial spy."

They marched for two more days and then camped at White Oak Bayou (in what is now part of the city of Houston). During the night, Erastus "Deaf" Smith, one of the general's best scouts and spies, captured two Hispanic men and brought them to camp. They said they were Tejanos who had lost their way and knew nothing about any troops. They were searched but nothing was found on them — at first.

Under armed guard, the two men were tied to a tree and given a rest after their first round of questioning. Kit hid in the bushes directly behind the tree and listened as the two prisoners whispered to each other. He picked up just enough information to know that Mexican forces had burned the town of Harrisburg eight miles away.

He rushed over to Jack and said, "These guys aren't just peasants. They know more than they're letting on."

After intense questioning, the two men were searched again. This time in a hollowed-out boot, Coker and Smith discovered a map and battle plans that had been intended for another of Santa Anna's generals. The hidden message revealed that the Mexican troops had gone down the west side of Buffalo Bayou where it meets the San Jacinto River, and that Santa Anna was personally in command.

"Kit, you did a great job of spyin'," said Coker.

"Can I join your army now?" Kit asked eagerly.

"When Santa Anna comes a-skipping into our camp and does a little jig for us, then you can join up," Coker replied with a grin.

Coker's expression turned somber when Smith told him, "We're moving out to Buffalo Bayou. We're not going to retreat anymore. We're going to take the fight to Santa Anna."

Two days later, Houston's men, now numbering about 900 strong, made camp about a mile from Santa Anna's forces. As Kit ate a plate of beans, he overheard Coker talking strategy with Deaf Smith. "Santa Anna had to cross the bridge over Sims Bayou because the water is so deep from all the rain we've been having. That means he and his men would have to cross the same bridge in retreat. But what if there wasn't a bridge anymore? Then he'd have no way to escape and no reinforcements could reach him because they would have no way of crossing, either."

"Why, Coker, I had no idea there were any brains under that coonskin hat of yours," said Smith.

So Smith went to General Houston with Coker's suggestion to destroy the bridge. Houston liked the idea and ordered Smith to get his six best men to carry out the mission, which meant they had to skirt by the Mexican camp to get to the bridge and then return without being seen.

"Can I go with you?" Kit asked Coker.

"Not on your life," he replied. "Now stay put. That's an order."

But Kit didn't stay. Early the next morning on April 21, 1836, Smith and his men headed out on their assignment. Without them knowing it, Kit tried to follow them. He lost their trail when he realized he had walked almost to the edge of the Mexicans' camp.

Hiding in the thick brush, he gasped at the sight. There was Santa Anna's army resting in a clearing behind a hill next to a marsh. Trunks, baggage, saddles, and other equipment were piled up to provide needed cover for the troops. *I've never seen so many soldiers in my life,* thought Kit. *There must be twice as many as Houston's.*

If the soldiers were preparing for battle, they didn't seem very tense or in a hurry. They laughed and kidded as they went about their tasks. Kit was filled with contrasting feelings — fear and fascination from seeing such a large enemy force. He sensed he was about to witness a historic event. He hoped only that the outcome would be a good one for Texas.

I shouldn't be here, Kit told himself. *I could be in big trouble if I'm captured or if the general finds out about this.* Just as he was about to leave, he heard a twig snap. *Someone is coming.*

Off to his right in the shadow of the trees he saw a figure moving toward the camp. Kit relaxed when he recognized the person as one of Houston's spies, obviously gathering vital information for the impending invasion. In a weird way, Kit thought it was funny that he felt compelled to hide from both the Mexicans and the Texans.

As the spy crept forward, Kit noticed, out of the corner of his eye, a Mexican soldier chasing after a wild turkey that was scurrying right toward the spy. *Oh no, if he spots our spy and warns the Mexicans, there won't be a surprise attack.* Kit quickly picked up a rock. If ever he needed a perfect aim, this was the time. From behind a tree, he hurled the rock at the turkey and struck it in the side of the breast. The big bird let out a squawk and then turned around and raced past the soldier and toward the Mexicans' camp. The soldier ran after the turkey, not knowing how close he came to discovering Houston's spy. Meanwhile, the spy continued his mission, not knowing that it was Kit who had saved him from being detected.

That's too close a call, thought Kit. He scurried back to Houston's camp. A short while later, Deaf Smith and his men returned with great news: They had destroyed the bridge by burning it.

By early afternoon, Houston's men were itching to fight — and in good humor. "If you get bumped off, Coker, won't you will me your coonskin cap?" asked one of the soldiers from his company.

Coker whipped it off his head and threw it at him. "You can take the cap now; I'll be wearing a Mexican officer's hat by the end of the day."

The soldier threw the cap back to Coker. "You better wear it in battle otherwise the sun bouncing off that bare head of yours will blind us all."

In the middle of the afternoon, when it was time to march on Santa Anna's forces, General Houston sat atop his horse and bellowed, "Remember, my boys, you are fighting for Texas and your loved ones, to avenge the inhuman butchery of your friends and comrades at the Alamo and at Goliad! The spirits of those brave men call to us for revenge. Remember your wives and little children who are now in flight to escape the fury of the ruthless invaders. . . . The time is here and we will win if everyone does his duty. We must win or die. Let us fight fast and hard!"

When they reached the edge of the Mexicans' camp, Houston gave the order to attack. The Texans charged out of the woods, surprising the Mexicans who were just rising from their afternoon siesta. Yelling "Remember the Alamo! Remember Goliad!" the *diablos tejanos* (Texas Devils, as the Mexicans called them) used their guns, swords, knives, and hand-to-hand combat to completely rout the enemy.

It was all over in less than twenty minutes.

The casualties, according to Houston's official report: 630 Mexicans killed, 208 wounded, and 730 taken prisoner; only nine Texans were killed and thirty wounded. The next day Santa Anna was captured. The Battle of San Jacinto would ultimately end the revolution of 1836 and establish Texas as a free republic.

The day after the attack, the victorious Texans gathered up the spoils of war — muskets, pistols, sabers, mules, horses, provisions, clothing, tents, and silver. Kit went over to the area where the prisoners were kept.

He instantly recognized one of the captured officers as the colonel who was in the cabin the night Kit was hiding in the loft. Given permission to speak to him, Kit proudly told him, "Do you remember when you were in a cabin about a week ago going over plans to launch a surprise attack against Houston? Well, I was spying on you, and that's why your plan failed."

The colonel spit on the ground in disgust, and with cutting sarcasm, told Kit, "If I had known you were spying in the attic, there would have been one less Texas rat in that cabin."

Although nothing more is known about him, Kit Benson, like all the brave soldiers who fought at the Battle of San Jacinto, took pride in helping — in his own modest way — achieve Texas liberty. The victory changed the map of North America and established the independent Lone Star Republic of Texas. Nine years later, Texas became the country's twenty-eighth state.

– The –
Newsboy

Charles Phillips, Union Spy
Civil War

1863–1865

"**R**ead all about it!" shouted the paperboy. "Unknown scoundrel tries to burn down the Presidential Mansion!"

Fourteen-year-old Charles Phillips hollered out the headlines while walking among rebel soldiers who were manning one of the many small forts that guarded Richmond, Virginia. It wasn't uncommon during this distressing time of civil war that the capital of the Confederate States of America – where its president, Jefferson Davis, lived – was the target of sabotage.

"Villain's efforts to set fire to the President's house sends smoke pouring out of the basement!" shouted Charles. With every word, puffs of his frosty breath floated in the brisk January morning. "Read all about it!"

"Boy! Over here!" yelled a grizzled soldier who was leaning

against a cannon. "I'll buy one!" He flipped a coin to Charles who snatched it out of the air and then handed the rebel a copy of *The Richmond Dispatch.* "I'm starving for some news."

"There's a good story about the Yankee prisoners who were captured after escaping from Castle Thunder," said Charles. He sat down next to the soldier and began chatting with him about the confederate defenses. "What I've seen, there's no way the Yankees can bust through these defenses."

The soldier shook his head. "I'm not so sure. I was on courier duty yesterday and went by a line of fortifications about three miles from here by the James River. Many heavy guns were in position. But darned if I didn't see a single soldier anywhere near those guns. Why, if the Yankees knew that, they'd sneak in and spike every one of them."

Charles knew exactly what the rebel meant — Union soldiers could easily sabotage the unmanned guns. Charles also knew exactly what to do with this information — relay it to the Yankees.

That's because the lanky, easygoing teenager was more than just a paperboy. He was a Union spy.

In 1863, Charles Phillips moved with his family to Richmond where his father John was hired to operate the presses for the *Dispatch.* John, whose sympathies lay with the North, soon began spying for the Union, collecting information from unsuspecting Confederate-supporting war correspondents. When John confided to his family that he was a spy, Charles asked eagerly, "Can I be one, too?"

"No, you're too young and you're much too nice to people,"

his father said. "This business is hazardous and is best left to the grown-ups. Besides, it requires nerves of steel and a high level of confidence that comes from experience."

The freckle-faced redhead went to his room and stewed. *What kind of baloney is that? I'm "too young" and "too nice." Hey, wait a minute. Too nice? That's it! I can strike up a conversation with anyone, even soldiers. Maybe I can get them to tell me things that could prove useful to the Union.* Charles was already earning money by selling newspapers all over town. So he decided to sell them in the local rebel encampments and chat with the soldiers, some of whom would likely talk too much and reveal vital bits of information. Not only that but he could report on gun placements, troop strength, and other intelligence about the camps that he visited.

Lugging his bag of papers, he went to a camp at the edge of town and tried his luck. Over dinner a few days later, Charles told his father, "I know what the rebels are doing on Brown's Island. Inside those buildings they have three hundred women making percussion caps, friction primers, fuses, signal lights, small arm cartridges, and artillery."

John dropped his fork in amazement. "How in the world do you know this?"

The boy grinned and replied, "Just being a good newsboy."

The following week, John sat down with Charles in front of their fireplace and said, "I've talked it over with the leader of our spy ring and she's agreed that you can work with us."

Charles leaped out of his chair. "That's great, Pa!" When he sat back down, his expression changed from joy to puzzled. "Who's your leader?"

John replied, "Elizabeth Van Lew."

"'Crazy Bet'? Pa, are you joshing me?"

"No, son. She's been spying for the Union ever since the war broke out."

"But she's just a loony, rich spinster."

"It's true she's a wealthy old maid, but she's not crazy. She's so smart she makes people think she's nuts."

Elizabeth Van Lew and her elderly mother, who were members of a wealthy Virginia family, lived in a three-story mansion in the middle of Richmond with several well-paid, educated former slaves. Even though she had no training, she chose on her own to create a spy network of everyday people from businessmen, tradesmen, servants, and even newsboys.

Townspeople called Miss Van Lew "Crazy Bet" because she seldom took care of her curled brown hair, wore old clothes that didn't match, donned battered bonnets, and openly talked about her support for the North. She did all she could to foster the impression that she was just a silly old woman who babbled nonsense. When she walked along the street, she would bend her head to one side and hold imaginary conversations.

Meeting her for the first time at her mansion atop Church Hill, Charles was surprised at how small Miss Van Lew was — shorter than him. Between high cheekbones and above a pointy nose, she had brilliant blue eyes that sparkled with passion and intelligence. Charles could tell they definitely weren't those of a crazy lady.

"I am criticized daily and told that I don't belong in Richmond," she told him. "But I am a good Southerner, holding to an old Virginian tradition of opposition to human bondage. I am the loyal one; they are the traitors. Slave power crushes freedom of speech and of opinion. Slave power degrades labor. Slave power is arrogant and cruel not only to the slave but to the community, the state, and the nation."

There was no need to give her little speech to Charles. Like his parents, he felt strongly that slavery was wrong and that everyone deserved to be free. That's why he believed the Confederacy had to be defeated.

Charles began as a courier for Miss Van Lew, who had established five secret relay stations between her home in Richmond and the Union lines. Members of her spy ring staffed these places, which were usually houses or businesses, and delivered messages swiftly to the Yankees.

Like the other couriers, Charles often carried a dispatch that had been torn in half. He hid one part of it in his shoe while the other part was given to another courier who took a different route to the Union lines. That way, if one part of the dispatch fell into enemy hands, they had nothing but half the paper with a lot of letters and numbers because all the messages were written in a special code, sometimes in invisible ink.

He often carried innocent-looking mail that appeared to exchange family news between a certain Miss Eliza Jones and her dear uncle James Jones, who lived in Union-occupied Norfolk, Virginia. In reality, these letters were intended for General Benjamin Butler at Fortress Monroe, outside of Norfolk. He knew that between the lines of each letter was information — written in invisible ink — about Confederate activities in Richmond. The undetected words became visible when the letter was dipped in milk.

When he wasn't working as a secret courier, Charles sold newspapers to rebel soldiers and engaged in small talk, hoping to learn important information. As a newsboy, he had to hustle to make money because he was competing against many others like Jim Smith and his younger brother, Tom. Born and raised in Richmond, the brothers — ages 14 and 12 — certainly weren't shy about who they supported in the war.

"Sometimes when I'm in a Union camp, I spit in the newspapers before I sell them to the Yankees," Tom said, flashing a sly grin.

"And I'll tear out part of an inside page so they can't get the full story," added Jim, who was as big and strong as their father, a fireman.

Usually when Charles, the Smith brothers, and the other newsboys sold all their papers, they got together and threw rocks at tin cans or flung stones from slingshots. Charles often wondered how many of them were spies like him. *I know one thing,* he thought. *If the Smith brothers are spies, they're definitely on the side of the South.*

One day, Charles was hawking his papers near the Libby Prison, a large block of former warehouses that held thousands of Union prisoners. As he sold copies of *The Richmond Dispatch* to rebel soldiers who were milling around outside, he sensed a buzz in the air. Groups of soldiers were talking in hushed but excited tones. He picked up bits and pieces: "thousands are going" . . . "moving 'em to Georgia" . . . "Andersonville" . . .

I need to find out what's going on, Charles thought.

"Read all about it! Yankee prisoners escape from Cary Street Prison!" he shouted. "Read all about it!"

One of the soldiers motioned him over and said, "How'd they do it, boy?"

"Why don't you buy a paper and find out?" Charles replied.

"Don't have the money. C'mon, how'd they escape?"

Charles read part of the story out loud to the soldier: "Between twelve o'clock Thursday night and yesterday morning, eighteen Yankee prisoners, confined in the prison on Cary Street opposite Castle Thunder, made their escape. They cut through the wall into the commissary storehouse next door and then went out the window and on to the street below. This breakout happened because the prison guards were not alert."

The soldier laughed and said, "Well, that's not gonna happen here at Libby."

"Why do you say that?" asked Charles.

"Because this prison is going to be emptied out."

"What do you mean?"

"We're moving thousands of them out of here to that big prison camp in Andersonville, Georgia."

This could be very important news, Charles thought. *I wonder if the Union knows about this.* "When is this going to happen?" he asked the soldier.

"Soon. Say, what else is making news in that rag of yours?"

Reading from another front-page story, Charles said, "It says here that Mr. Ingram, the former owner of the St. Charles Hotel, was captured by the Yankees in Richmond County, last week. He was buying bacon and other supplies for the Confederacy when he was caught. Well, I better go sell some more papers."

Charles raced straight to Miss Van Lew's home and told her about the planned prison transfer. "What an interesting development," she said. "If it's true, this could be an opportunity· for a sudden Northern attack, one that could free a great many Union prisoners. Why, the Union might even take Richmond!"

By the end of the day, her best spies in the city confirmed Charles's information and uncovered even more details about the transfer as well as troop movements in and around Richmond.

Miss Van Lew wrote a dispatch in code and invisible ink and then, with John Phillips's approval, agreed to send Charles to deliver it to General Butler's headquarters 100 miles away. At the last minute, new intelligence from her best spies arrived at her house, so she gave the information verbally to Charles for him to memorize and pass on to the general.

Armed with a Confederate pass, Charles and one of Miss Van Lew's servants took a horse-drawn buggy to Fortress Monroe. On their arrival three days later, Charles showed General Butler a token — a three-leaf clover carved into the center of a peach pit — that proved the boy was a trusted member of the Van Lew spy ring. Then Charles recited the information he had memorized and handed the general Miss Van Lew's dispatch.

"Well done, lad," commended the general. "Based on this information, it's obvious to me that the time to strike Richmond is now when it appears to be the most vulnerable."

When Charles returned to Richmond, he learned that the dispatch had been immediately forwarded to Washington, DC, where Union officials prepared for a major military operation. The War Department hoped to surprise Richmond and free the prisoners. Unfortunately for the Union, the rebel soldiers were ready and successfully defended the city against the attack, forcing the Yankees to retreat.

A few days later, Charles bumped into the Smith brothers at a Confederate encampment where they were selling newspapers to the soldiers. "The boys sure whupped them Yankees," gloated Jim.

"Yep," said Charles, doing his best to hide his disappointment.

"It was like swatting flies," added Tom. "The Yankees didn't stand a chance, not after our side already knew their attack plans ahead of time."

"Are you saying Confederate spies warned the army here? How would you know?"

"Our father is on General Lee's personal staff, so he . . ."

"Keep your trap shut, Tom," snapped Jim.

"No need to worry," Charles said. "I'm for the South, of course."

"Oh, yeah?" challenged Jim. "Then why have we seen you hanging around Crazy Bet's house?"

Charles's face turned as red as his hair. "Have you been spying on me?"

"Nah, but we've seen you there more than once."

"I deliver her papers and sometimes I do errands for her," Charles explained. "She pays real well."

"Better stay away from her if you know what's good for you. She's one of those Yankee lovers."

"True," said Charles, "but we all know she's nuttier than a pecan pie."

Charles made a mental note to be more careful in case the Smith brothers followed him. But that didn't stop him from sometimes guiding escaped Union prisoners to Miss Van Lew's house. She would hide them in secret chambers in her mansion until she made arrangements to get them back across Union lines.

One evening, Charles saw Miss Van Lew carrying a tray of food up to the attic. He was curious, so he tiptoed after her and saw her touch a wooden panel on the wall. To his surprise, it slid back, and a bearded man reached out hungrily for the food. The boy recognized him as one of the escaped prisoners he had brought to the mansion.

In late 1864, the need for military horses was so great in Richmond that owners were expected to donate their steeds to the Confederacy. Few people were allowed to keep their animals. While selling newspapers one day, Charles overheard a rebel soldier say that a squad was planning to seize Miss Van Lew's horse. The boy sprinted ahead to her house and warned her.

"The soldiers were here earlier this week," she said. "I was tipped off by one of our spies so I hid my horse in the smokehouse, and they didn't find him."

"You better hurry and do something because they'll be here in a few minutes," said Charles.

"Take him to my library," she ordered.

"In your house?" he asked in disbelief.

"Yes, the library on the second floor. Go, go."

With a little coaxing, Charles led the horse into the mansion and up the stairs to the library. Meanwhile, servants hurriedly brought in straw and spread it around the floor. Moments later, the soldiers arrived and searched the grounds and the smokehouse for the horse. They didn't bother to look in the mansion because they never considered that she would hide her horse there. When they left, she told Charles and the servants. "Did you see how good my horse was? He behaved as though he thoroughly understood matters. He never neighed or stamped loud enough to be heard. What a good, loyal horse he is."

When General Ulysses S. Grant and his Union troops moved closer to Richmond, communications between the Van Lew spy ring and the Northern army command was faster than ever. Messages were forwarded almost daily to the general using Miss Van Lew's relay system.

Charles begged her for a chance to meet Grant, the commander of all of the Union's troops and the North's most popular man next to President Abraham Lincoln. "When you come up with an important piece of information, I'll let you take it to him personally," she told the boy.

While selling newspapers in a small southeastern neighborhood, Charles noticed rebel soldiers and slaves building small fortifications connected by a series of breastworks. He also spotted two recently built magazines (storehouses for gunpowder and ammunition). Hiding in an alleyway, he carefully drew maps of these new defenses in a page of one of the newspapers he had stuffed in his bag.

This should get me the chance to meet with Grant, Charles thought.

He was right. Miss Van Lew was so impressed that she let him handle the final leg of the relay to the general's temporary headquarters, which were on the grounds of an estate near City Point, Virginia, southeast of Richmond.

In a small wooden building on the east lawn, Charles stood at attention in front of the somber, stocky military leader and proudly gave his report. The general stroked his brown beard, nodded, and mumbled, "Thank you, Master Charles. We'll put your information to good use."

As he turned to leave, Charles said, "Oh, one more thing, General." He reached into his bag and pulled out the morning edition of *The Richmond Dispatch*. "This is fresh off the presses." Then from the bag, he produced a bouquet of flowers. "And this is fresh from Miss Van Lew's garden." The general gave the boy the first hint of a smile.

When Charles stepped out of the building, he was stunned to see the Smith brothers selling papers. He spun to his left and walked briskly — but not so fast that he would draw attention — to a nearby wagon and hid behind it. *What dumb luck to have them selling papers here on the day I meet Grant,* he thought. *I hope they didn't see me coming out of his headquarters. They're already suspicious of me.*

After a few minutes, he got up and walked around the encampment, selling the rest of his papers. He hoped the Smith boys wouldn't spot him. As he started to leave, he heard a familiar voice: "Sold all your copies?"

Charles cringed and turned around. *Drat! It's them.* "Hey, Jim. Hey, Tom. What are you doing here?"

"Same as you, trying to make a little money," Jim replied.

"But you hate the Yankees," said Charles.

Tom shrugged and said, "We'll take their money any day."

"Well, boys, I got to get back home. See you later."

As he was leaving the camp, Charles was stopped by an aide to General George Sharpe, Grant's intelligence chief. "General Sharpe wants to see you in his tent," the aide told Charles.

Now what? After Charles was introduced, the general asked, "We saw you talking to those two newsboys. Do you know them?"

"Yes sir," Charles answered. "Jim and Tom Smith. They're brothers and definitely supporters of the Confederacy. In fact, their father is on General Lee's personal staff."

"Is that so? I've received word that they are trained spies. They've been traveling along our lines selling newspapers while they're spying. They're giving Lee all manner of information about us. They are sharp and do a thrifty business. Keep an eye on them for us, will you?"

"Yes, sir."

But Charles knew the more he spied on the brothers, the more they would spy on him. Over the next few weeks, their paths crossed a few times but no one acted in a suspicious manner. In fact, Charles made sure to take some slingshot target practice with them so they wouldn't think he was wary of them.

In January 1865, General Grant's troops began closing in on Richmond and Charles kept spying on the rebel encampments while selling his newspapers. After Miss Van Lew gave him a bottle of invisible ink, he used it for the first time to sketch the battery placements of a Confederate fort. He drew it on an inside page of a newspaper. Sitting against the trunk of an old oak, Charles was nearly finished when ... *pop!* ... a stone tore through the paper and struck him in the shoulder. Startled, he rose to his feet and saw the Smith brothers trotting over to him. Jim had a slingshot in his hand. Tom was carrying a small pail of milk.

"Hey, what'd you do that for?" Charles said. "I was reading the paper."

"Oh? What are you reading?" Jim snatched the paper out of Charles's hands, looked at it, and then casually dropped it into the milk pail, saying, "Oops."

Angrily, Charles started to fish it out but Jim grabbed his arm, spun him around, and then threw him down. Meanwhile, Tim pulled the paper out of the pail and held it up. "Well, lookee here," he said. "There's a drawing on this page. Sure looks just like the fort over there. Even the gun placements match up."

Jim, who had Charles pinned to the ground, said, "Seems you were doing more than just reading, pal."

An hour later Charles found himself locked up in a prison charged with spying, one of the youngest ever arrested.

About nine weeks later, on April 3, he watched from his third-floor cell as victorious Union soldiers marched into Richmond, many of its buildings set ablaze by retreating rebel forces. In the smoky city, Yankee bands played while Northern sympathizers, especially former slaves, cheered and danced in the streets.

Peering through the dark haze, Charles saw something that made him whoop and holler for joy. There atop Church Hill on the roof of a familiar mansion was Elizabeth Van Lew and her servants raising the American flag — the first to unfurl in the city that would no longer reign as the capital of the Confederacy.

Charles Phillips grew up knowing that he was a member of one of the Union's most effective spy rings ever, even though none of its spies and couriers had any formal training in espionage. Unfortunately, the full details of the spy ring will never be known. A year after the Civil War ended, the War Department turned over all documents and dispatches to Miss Van Lew at her request. She then burned all the papers. But at least history can record that she and all the members of her spy ring, including Charles Phillips, risked their lives to end slavery forever.

The
Rebel Joan of Arc

BELLE BOYD, CONFEDERATE SPY
CIVIL WAR

1861–1863

Belle Boyd paced back and forth in her dreary, musty cell in the Old Capitol Prison. The teenage beauty had been arrested several times before, but she always managed to sweet talk her way to freedom. But not this time. The enemy — the Union — had caught her red-handed, and now Belle had never felt more frightened or more alone.

I must be brave, she told herself. *I must be defiant.*

The cell door swung open and in stepped Colonel Lafayette Baker, chief of the United States Secret Service. Seeing Belle for the first time, he mockingly said to her, "So this is the celebrated rebel spy. I am glad to have such a distinguished person in our federal prison."

Belle glared at him, letting her rage wash out any fear she had about her fate.

The colonel's sarcastic smile swiftly changed to a stony glare. "I've come here to get you to make a free confession of what you've done against our cause," he said.

After a long silence, Belle replied, "When you've informed me on what grounds I've been arrested, and given me a copy of the charges, I'll make a statement."

"Miss Belle, you are in terrible trouble. You stand to be cooped up in this prison for a long time. Perhaps conditions will improve for you if you were to denounce the Confederacy and swear an oath of allegiance to the United States."

Belle hissed, "I hope that if I were ever forced to take that oath, my tongue would stick to the roof of my mouth. If I were ever forced to sign one line to show allegiance, I hope my arm falls paralyzed to my side." She turned her back to him and snapped, "I'm so disgusted, I can't stand your presence any longer!"

Baker stormed out of the cell, slamming the door in frustration.

Wrapping her fingers around the bars of the lone window, Belle gazed out onto the streets of Washington, DC. The last time she was in the nation's capital, she was sixteen and making her society debut. She had danced with young officers in their smart dress uniforms, had tea with members of the upper class, and was introduced to members of business and government.

She thought about how the road in her young life had taken so many twists and turns and led her from ballrooms to battlefields. But then, this was the Civil War, and she was a teenage Confederate spy.

* * *

The thrill of adventure coursed through the veins of Maria Isabelle Boyd, daughter of Ben Boyd, owner of a store and tobacco farm in the beautiful Shenandoah Valley. Growing up in what is now Martinsburg, West Virginia, Belle was a wild tomboy who climbed trees, explored woods, and raced horses. Dominating her brothers and sisters, the feisty, tart-tongued girl was seldom disciplined by her mild-mannered mother.

At the age of 12, Belle was sent to the Mount Washington Female College in Baltimore. Four years later the tall, blue-eyed, brown-haired girl made her society debut in Washington. Prominent friends and relatives introduced the charming, outgoing teenager to the proper hostesses, guaranteeing invitations to the best affairs. Her life was a whirl of waltzes and cotillions, teas and parties, and breezy conversations with the best and the brightest.

But then early in 1861, 11 Southern states seceded from the Union to form the Confederate States of America, triggering the Civil War. It changed her life.

Belle returned home to West Virginia, which was then in Confederate territory, and made clear where she stood. "I am enthusiastic in my love for my country — the South," declared the teenager, who began raising money for the war effort by throwing parties. She praised her father, who despite being out of shape and 44 years old, volunteered for military service.

In July, her father's regiment battled Union forces near Belle's home. She had anticipated a great Confederate victory, but Belle watched with gloom as the rebel troops were forced to retreat through her hometown.

With her beloved Shenandoah Valley now under Union

control, she volunteered at the local hospital. While Belle was in a large ward tending to wounded Confederate soldiers, a triumphant Union officer marched in, waved the Stars and Stripes, and shouted, "You damned rebels can't lick anyone who fights under Old Glory."

Belle retorted, "How brave of a man can you be by insulting injured soldiers who are as helpless as babies."

Taken by surprise, the soldier asked, "And, pray tell, who might you be, miss?"

Belle replied, "A rebel lady — and proud of it."

Later, victorious Union soldiers smashed windows at random and broke into houses to hunt for Confederate souvenirs. Learning that the brassy teenager kept Confederate flags on the walls of her room, several troops stormed the Boyd home. They tore down pictures and knocked over vases. When a soldier climbed onto the roof and tried to hoist the American flag over the house, it was more than Belle could stand. In her outraged effort to stop him, she caused a near riot in which Union soldiers fired at the house and threatened to burn it down.

The Union commanding officer held a hearing in which Belle, faking tears and remorse, was cleared of any wrongdoing.

It was then that Belle decided to become a spy. Being a flirt and a good actress, she figured if she was friendly with Union soldiers, they might let slip some piece of information that could prove helpful to rebel commanders. She knew that being friendly with the enemy would anger many townspeople who were Southern sympathizers, but she was willing to tolerate their wrath for the good of the cause.

Whenever the amateur secret agent learned anything, she

wrote it down and sent it to General Stonewall Jackson or General Jeb Stuart. But being such a rookie in espionage, Belle was careless. She didn't write in code or make any effort to disguise her handwriting. So when one of her notes was intercepted, she was brought into a tent of Union officers.

"Miss Belle," said the colonel in command, "are you aware that by writing this note and trying to send it to the enemy, you could be considered a spy and might be sentenced to death?"

Too brash to be scared, Belle made a full curtsy and, with sarcasm dripping from her tongue, told the officers, "I have not been formally charged with any crime and yet you have tried and convicted me of spying within minutes of my visit. Well, thank you, gentlemen of the jury." And then she boldly walked out, wondering what would happen next. To her relief, nothing did.

I have to be much more careful from now on, she told herself.

For a while, she would fold a note until it was small enough to fit into a big watch that had its workings removed. Her maid, Sophie, who wore the watch, would walk to the nearest Confederate commander and deliver Belle's message. Sometimes the secret dispatch was hidden in a basket or even in the bun of Sophie's pulled-back hair.

Belle sought out Colonel Turner Ashby, head of rebel military scouts in the Shenandoah Valley, and offered her services as a spy. Ashby often conducted his own espionage by wearing civilian clothes and riding to Union camps, pretending to be a veterinarian. He would treat ailing horses, then return to his own lines with important information about the enemy.

Belle received several assignments from Ashby as a courier

for the Confederate forces. She learned the use of a cipher, a system based on a code word that could vary from message to message. Because of shifting battle zones, she frequently carried messages on brief runs on her horse through the backcountry.

In March 1862, Union officers arrested Belle after a double agent betrayed her. As she was led under armed guard to a Baltimore-bound train, she told rebel sympathizers, "Oh, don't be so glum. Nothing is going to happen to me. You'll see." She adjusted her brightly colored, beribboned hat and waved to her friends, showing the calmness of a woman going on a trip to see her relatives.

On the way to Baltimore, Belle waved a Confederate flag out the train window in every town the train went through. Instead of prison, she was kept in a comfortable hotel where she charmed her captors with her Southern wit and chatty friendliness. She remained there for a week before officials concluded that they didn't have enough evidence to charge her as a rebel spy. Major General John Dix let her leave, but not before giving her a fatherly warning to "avoid even the slightest appearance of being involved with espionage." She responded with a curtsy.

Belle rejoined her family forty miles south of their farm in the town of Front Royal, Virginia, where her aunt and uncle owned a small hotel. To her utter dismay, the area was under control of the Yankees. Officers had taken over the hotel, forcing her and her family to live in a cramped cottage nearby.

One night, Belle learned from a Union soldier whom she had befriended that a war council headed by General James

Shields was underway in the hotel parlor. She sneaked into an upstairs bedroom closet directly above the parlor and pried open a small knothole in a floorboard. Lying on the floor, she put her ear to the opening and listened for hours to every word as the men studied maps and debated strategy.

Belle tried to memorize names, figures, and placement of troops even though there was much she didn't understand. One thing she did understand was that Shields planned to surround Stonewall Jackson and his men and take him prisoner by combining regiments from other parts of the valley. After the meeting ended at one o'clock in the morning, she waited for the halls to clear before tiptoeing to her cottage and writing down her notes of what she had overheard. She tucked them in the sleeve of her dress. In her pocket, she slipped a pass that she had obtained from a paroled Confederate soldier.

Then she saddled her horse and galloped toward rebel lines. On her way, she was halted by a Union sentry.

"Now why would a young girl be out in the wee hour of the morning?" he asked.

She showed him the pass and, calling up fake tears, whined, "I just received word that my grandmother is on her deathbed. Please, I must hurry."

He motioned for her to go on. She had to repeat her little act in front of a second sentry before speeding across fields and streams for fifteen miles until she reached a safe house. Breathless, she jumped from her horse and pounded on the door. Colonel Ashby opened the door and exclaimed, "Good God! Miss Belle, is that you?"

After she gave him her notes, he thanked her and promised

to get this latest intelligence to Stonewall Jackson right away. Belle rode off, hoping to get back home before dawn. About a mile from the family cottage, she galloped past a drowsy sentry, who was so startled that he fired a shot at her but missed. By the time she plopped on her bed, exhausted, Shields's forces began moving out to confront Jackson's men.

Later that day, Belle persuaded a young Union lieutenant to escort her and her maid, Sophie, to the town of Winchester to "visit relatives" for the day. The trip was really for Belle to check out Union troop movements north of Front Royal. Shortly after they arrived, she walked out of sight of the officer and secretly met with a fellow agent.

"I have several important papers that you must get to Stonewall immediately," he whispered to her. Into her hands, he shoved four envelopes containing information dealing with the impending clash between Confederate and Union forces. Minutes later, she hid the document of greatest significance in her dress and gave the next most important paper to Sophie, figuring that a sentry wouldn't search a maid. Of the two least important documents, she put one in Sophie's basket and boldly gave the other to the clueless lieutenant to hold.

But on their way out of town, they were stopped by the Secret Service and taken to the Union colonel in charge in Winchester. He asked her, "Miss Belle, are you carrying any disloyal messages?"

"Why, heavens no," she replied, acting shocked at such a question. Knowing that the colonel would easily find the envelope in the basket, she lied, "I was given two packets by a gentleman I had never seen before. He asked me to do him a favor and deliver them to the hotel in Front Royal for a friend of his to pick up later. One of the packets is in the basket there."

"And the other one?" asked the colonel.

The flustered lieutenant hemmed and hawed before pulling the other envelope out of his pocket.

When the colonel read the papers, he exploded in a fury. "These are for the rebels!" Turning to the lieutenant, he shouted, "What kind of idiot are you, carrying messages for the rebels?!"

Thanks to her uncanny knack for faking innocence, Belle and her maid were allowed to leave. The lieutenant was arrested. Returning to Front Royal, the teenage agent was extremely pleased that she still possessed the two most important documents, the one she had hidden in her dress, and the one Sophie had concealed.

Reading the documents that she had been given in Winchester, Belle learned the battle plans of Union generals Nathaniel Banks, Julius White, and John Fremont who were combining forces to attack Stonewall Jackson's troops near Front Royal.

"I've got to warn Stonewall or he'll be defeated," she told Sophie.

"But the fighting has already started," said the maid. "You can't go out on the battlefield. You'll be killed."

"If I don't, Stonewall and his men are likely to be killed."

Belle stuffed the dispatches in the pockets of her blue dress, put on her white bonnet, and hurried toward the battlefield, coming up from behind the Union lines. On her way, she saw several Yankee soldiers running past her in the opposite direction. Spotting a soldier with whom she had enjoyed a pleasant conversation a few days earlier, she ran alongside him and asked, "What's happening?"

Without stopping, the soldier said, "We're beginning a retreat and plan to burn our stores [supplies]. We'll fight as best we can but once we get across the river, we're going to fire [burn] the bridges. Miss Belle, it's best you get out of here for your own good."

Ignoring his advice, Belle turned around and headed toward the front lines. She hurried past the Union soldiers and their heavy guns and equipment. She hoped they would be so focused on fighting the rebels that they wouldn't pay any attention to her as she walked briskly along the edge of the battlefield.

When she finally reached a meadow, Belle took off in a desperate sprint, but within seconds bullets began whizzing by her left and right. *They're shooting at me!* Trying to become a more difficult target, she zigzagged in her mad dash toward the other side, running faster than she ever had as a tomboy.

Hearing the whining of an incoming artillery shell, Belle threw herself on the ground just moments before it exploded a few yards from her. After dirt and rocks rained down on her, she got up and ran even faster, fueled by a combination of sheer terror and determination. She scrambled under fences and over rocks until she neared the rebel lines.

Waving her white bonnet, she caught the eye of Major Harry Douglas, who had known her since she was a little girl. He ran out to meet her.

"Great God, Belle, why are you here?"

After catching her breath, Belle blurted, "The Yankees are planning to retreat and burn the bridges. And I have some important dispatches for Stonewall that he needs to see immediately." As she pulled them out of her pockets, she realized that her pretty dress had been pockmarked with several bullet holes. Trying to joke to cover the frightening thought that she could have been killed, she said, "Those Yankees are bad shots. I guess I'll have some mending to do when I get back home."

Major Douglas took the documents from her. "I'll get this to Stonewall right away and tell him about the bridges. Belle, it's not safe here. Go back, but take the long way around."

Thanks to the intelligence that Belle had bravely delivered, General Jackson quickly changed his strategy and drove the Union forces back through Front Royal. During the battle, he also sent a special detachment to try to prevent the destruction of the bridges, which the Yankees had set on fire. Battling smoke and flames, the Confederates pulled down scorching timbers and tossed them into the water and were able to save the bridges.

When the day's combat ended, Major Douglas rode through town. Seeing him, Belle called him over and congratulated him on the victory. "Thank you," said the major. "You had an important role to play in our success, Miss Belle."

"I have something for you, Major." She held up a crimson rose and, as he leaned down from his saddle, she pinned it to his uniform. "I picked it because it's bloodred," she said. "It's my favorite color."

Jackson's forces went on to attack General Banks's troops and chased them in a rout through Winchester and north to the Potomac River. In this victorious campaign, Jackson's troops captured three thousand prisoners, thousands of small arms, and hundreds of thousands of dollars worth of supplies that the Union army didn't have time to destroy.

About a week later, Belle received a hand-delivered note from Jackson that was dated May 29. It read:

My dear Miss Belle:
I thank you, for myself and for the Army, for the immense service that you have rendered your country today.
Hastily, I am your friend,
T.J. Jackson, C.S.A.

With other battles to wage, the Confederates abandoned Front Royal and it soon fell back into Union hands, so Belle continued her undercover work as a secret agent.

One day she met a handsome young man in a Confederate uniform. He told her his name was John Daley and that he had been captured by the Yankees but was given a parole. He was waiting for a pass from them so he could return to his home in Virginia.

Having an instant crush on him, the teenager had him over for dinner with her family. Later, at her invitation, he accompanied her to a party where they laughed and danced and even sang a duet. During a romantic walk home, she whispered to him, "On your way to your hometown, could you deliver a dispatch to Stonewall for me?"

"Of course I will," he said.

After Belle went home to prepare the dispatch, Sophie warned her, "Miss Belle, you better watch out. I don't trust that

John Daley. I saw him talking to some Yankees today, and they were all mighty friendly."

"Oh, don't be ridiculous," said Belle. "He's a Southern gentleman."

But before she gave him the dispatch, Belle asked him bluntly, "There's a rumor going around that you're a Union spy. Are you?"

"Miss Belle, I assure you my allegiance is with the Confederacy."

"I believe you," she said.

What she didn't know was that John Daley was really C.W.D. Smitley, a member of Jessie's Scouts, a secret group of Union spies who dressed in Confederate uniforms.

Shortly after he left town, Union officers showed up at Belle's house and announced they were conducting an investigation. Belle and her relatives were lined up against a wall as the officers began a search of the house. They were unaware that in another room Sophie had frantically but quietly gathered a handful of Belle's records and sneaked out. Away from the house, she burned the documents.

Meanwhile, during the search, the officers broke open a desk and found other papers that clearly showed Belle was more than just a friendly teenage Southern girl. "Miss Belle, you are under arrest for being a Confederate spy," said one of the officers. Unlike previous arrests, this time the Union had strong evidence. She knew her wit, charm, and boldness weren't going to help her get out of this dilemma. As she was led away through a crowd, Southern sympathizers cheered her while Northern supporters jeered her.

After Belle was put on a train for a prison in Washington, the brave face that she had always displayed suddenly scrunched into sorrow and she cried. She wept not only because she was in serious trouble, but because she had been betrayed by someone she had fallen for.

However, by the time she was thrown into the Old Capitol Prison, she was once again her brash, defiant self. She refused to answer any questions about her spying and instead acted less like a prisoner and more like a fun-loving Southern belle at an afternoon tea, much to the frustration of her captors.

She did not hide her affection for the Confederacy and often sang "Dixie" at the top of her lungs, encouraging other prisoners to join in. She sang other songs about the South with such conviction and emotion that she moved many fellow rebels to tears. She had become so famous the press called her the "Rebel Joan of Arc" and the "Siren of the Shenandoah."

Eventually, officials sent Belle and several other inmates to Richmond as part of a prisoner exchange. In the capital of the Confederacy, Belle, whose spying days were now over, was treated as a heroine. Generals visited her and strangers stopped her on the street to praise her. Stonewall Jackson even made her an honorary member of his staff with the rank of captain for the intelligence she provided in the capture of Front Royal.

At a reception in her honor, she told her admirers, "It wasn't so much that I wanted to be a spy. It was that I wanted to help my people."

"You have!" shouted a supporter. "You most definitely have!"

At the age of 20, Belle moved to England and wrote a book about her espionage experiences called Belle Boyd in Camp and Prison *and gave readings on the British stage. When she returned to the United States, she continued her stage readings, billing herself as the "Cleopatra of the Secession." Belle, who was married three times, died in 1900 in Wisconsin. Her legacy lives on as the most colorful spy the South ever had.*

— The —
Slave Boy

Crack! Charley Felton winced as he felt the sting of the horsehide whip slash across the back of his bare legs.

Crack! "No slave of mine runs away without paying for it with a pound of flesh," bellowed plantation owner Robert Felton. *Crack!* Two other slaves, who had been ordered to tie the young slave's arms to a fence and pull down his pants, looked on helplessly. Felton turned to them and warned, "The same will happen to you if you even *think* about escaping. Now untie him and get back to work!"

Charley slumped to the ground, his calves bleeding and swollen from the whipping. Despite the pain, he was proud that he hadn't uttered a single sound in anguish. He didn't want to give his cruel master the satisfaction.

The next time I run away from here, I will not get caught,

Charley vowed. *And I* will *run away again. The Union lines aren't that far from here.*

His brief taste of freedom — he was caught just a day after he took off — made him hunger even more for liberty. In all his sixteen years, his whole world revolved around the 300-acre plantation in eastern North Carolina where he was told what to do and when to do it. He toiled in fields of wheat, rye, and oats; lived in a drafty shack with his mother and two younger sisters; and drank mostly thick sour milk, and ate hoe cakes (similar to corn bread), vegetables, and scraps of meat and fat that the owner's family didn't want.

Charley's hopes for freedom were boosted by news that Union forces were winning battles against the Confederates in the region. He was feeling especially good in early 1862 when he learned that the Yankees had captured New Bern, North Carolina, about fifty miles away from the Felton plantation. Because the Union was accepting and protecting all escaping slaves who could make it safely across its lines, hundreds of runaways were pouring into the town.

He heard that if he could reach the Union side, he would be given food and shelter and a job with pay. Former slaves were earning up to ten dollars a month for the Yankees by raising crops, building forts, and acting as guides, scouts, and spies.

Charley hoped that one day he, too, could be a spy for the Union. In the meantime, he wanted to do his part to defeat the Confederates and end slavery.

One day, he and several other slaves were ordered to dig a big hole behind the stables. Late in the afternoon, George Winslow, who owned a plantation several miles away, arrived with his slaves and two wagons loaded with heavy crates. Following orders, the slaves lowered the wooden boxes in the hole and covered them up.

No one knew what was in the crates, but Charley was determined to find out. That evening, he sneaked under the open window of the mansion behind a rain barrel and listened as his master and Winslow smoked cigars. Charley had heard through the grapevine that Winslow had given large sums of money to the Confederacy.

"You have no idea of the danger we face from the Negroes," Felton told Winslow. "They think Abraham Lincoln is going to set them free."

"What do they know about Lincoln? They're illiterate slaves."

"They have their ways of passing information down from the North. They know as much about what is happening in Washington as we do — and too much for our own safety. We must never talk about the war in front of them."

"Would you like to hear my latest plan?" Winslow asked.

"More guns to hide on my land?"

"No, a more inventive scheme. I plan to fill a commissary wagon with poisoned water. The wagon will be broken and left abandoned on the side of the road north of Frederick to make it easy for the Yankees to find it. Naturally, they'll start drinking it and then —" he started to chortle — "they will die a horrible death."

"You do have a twisted mind, Winslow. Clever, but twisted."

Charley couldn't believe his good fortune. He learned not only about the hidden guns — no doubt for the rebels who might be passing through — but also an evil plan to poison Union troops.

In his eagerness to tell someone about the results of his spying, he tripped over a pail next to the rain barrel, causing Felton and Winslow to run to the window. Charley dived behind a bush and then began yowling and hissing.

"Just a couple of tomcats wrestling around out there," said Felton.

When the coast was clear, Charley scurried over to the cabin that housed the plantation's single male slaves. He woke up Joe Clark, a tall, 35-year-old slave who had become a father figure to Charley after the boy's dad was killed in a farm accident ten years before.

After explaining what he had heard, Charley said, "I've got to get word to the Union, but how?"

"Same way that you get news from the North."

"I don't understand, Joe."

"Well, it's about time I let you in on a secret, boy."

Joe got a written pass from his master so he and Charley could pick up supplies in town for the plantation. Late in the afternoon, they made a detour to the edge of a nearby farm where a two-story rundown wooden building stood. Joe knocked three times before he and Charley entered. Once inside, they heard muffled voices and the shuffling of feet above them.

"Who comes?" someone shouted down.

"Friends of Uncle Abe," Joe replied.

"What do you desire?"

"Light and liberty."

Immediately, a trapdoor overhead opened and a rope ladder dropped down. Following Joe up the ladder, Charley entered a dark, barren room lit by a single candle that gave shadowy glimpses of a dozen black men of all ages. The only furniture was an overturned barrel with an American flag draped over it.

After exchanging greetings with them, Joe announced, "This here is Charley. I vouch for him. He's trustworthy and a smart boy. Done some readin', writin', and 'rithmetic. Makes a darn good spy, too. Tell 'em what you know, boy."

After Charley briefed them, the leader — a husky, gray-haired man — said, "We'll send someone to warn the Yankees about the poison and we'll tell them about Felton's hidden guns. Boy, you've helped the cause."

"We best get going," said Joe, "because if we're late, our backs will look like raw meat."

As they headed toward the Felton plantation, Charley asked, "Who were those men?"

"Why, that was the local chapter of the Legal League. That's a secret group of slaves with hideouts all over the South. They help escaped slaves and prisoners and pass on information to friends and soldiers of the Union. That's how we get our news. And they do some spyin' and sometimes they do things like 'accidentally' start a fire or 'accidentally' break a piece of machinery on their plantation if it'll help slow down the rebels."

"Do the Confederates know about the Legal League?"

"Probably not. We slaves are supposed to be dumber than dirt. We couldn't possibly be so clever as to have a secret network throughout the South. We're countin' on the rebs to keep thinkin' like that."

"Will the Legal League help me escape?" Charley asked.

"Probably. But be patient, boy. Be patient."

Over the next few weeks, more shipments of guns for the Confederacy arrived and were buried on the plantation. But every time Charley wanted to plan an escape, Joe kept saying, "Not until we find out where the guns are comin' from."

What few chances Charley had to eavesdrop outside the window proved fruitless. He was getting antsy, yearning to escape, and believed that with every passing day it was getting harder to flee. With an increasing number of battles between Confederate and Union troops, many plantation owners were sending their slaves for safekeeping to Richmond, Virginia, the capital of the Confederacy.

A growing uneasiness crept over those who were left behind on the Felton plantation because it was extremely difficult now to run away. Pattie rollers — posses of armed white men — rode from plantation to plantation every night now, stopping black people, searching their homes for smuggled goods, and whipping any slave caught traveling without a written pass.

Charley was cleaning the saddles one night when the slave master ordered, "Boy, get out here and bring me some short ropes."

Uh-oh, someone's in trouble, Charley thought. *I hope it's not me.*

When he came out with the ropes, Charley saw that two pattie rollers were holding up a tall slave who, judging from his limp body, had been beaten. In front of them were Felton and the slave master. "Tie him to the fence and take down his pants," Felton ordered.

As he stepped closer, Charley cringed. In the flickering light of the torch he could see that the slave who was about to get whipped had a swollen face and was bleeding. The boy could barely make out who it was. *Oh, no! It's Joe! He looks so bad the whipping might kill him. I can't tie him up.*

"Faster, boy, or you'll feel the sting, too," said the slave master.

Sensing what was going on in Charley's head, Joe mumbled to him, "Just do it."

Reluctantly, Charley tied Joe's hands to the fence and stepped back, casting his eyes away as Felton whipped Joe over and over until the slave was unconscious. "Leave him there," Felton said. "If he's alive in the morning, then you can get him."

Charley didn't wait until morning. Once everyone went to sleep, he untied Joe and gave him some water. Then he and another slave, David, carried him to the slave quarters and nursed him through the night.

The next morning, Joe stirred and moaned. Looking up through swollen eyes, he saw Charley and smiled. Although it was hard for him to speak, he murmured, "Time . . . to . . . leave . . . this . . . life."

"Are you going to die?" Charley asked with alarm.

Joe shook his head. "Know . . . where . . . guns . . . come . . . from."

When Joe recovered enough to speak clearly, he explained that he had followed Winslow to his plantation and heard him talking to a fellow Confederate about a rebel gunrunning scheme. Two wealthy men named Hudson and Franklin from Baltimore would buy supplies and put them on a ship bound for

Europe. Guns for the rebels were hidden in the crates. Outside Virginia Beach, Virginia, the ship would anchor and the supplies transferred to a smaller boat that would deliver the contraband to North Carolina. Meanwhile, the ship would sail on and, if stopped and searched by Union gunboats, would be free of any smuggled weapons.

"On my way back from Winslow's the pattie rollers got me," Joe said. "Get word to the Legal League and let's plan our getaway."

A few nights later, at the league's next secret meeting, Charley showed up and relayed Joe's information. During the session, Charley learned that Union gunboats were patrolling up and down the Pamlico River nearby.

As soon as Joe was able to walk, Charley, Joe, and David sneaked out of the plantation late at night and made their way to the river, waiting for a gunboat to pass. They knew they had only a few hours before the slave master would discover they were missing and send out the pattie rollers. If a gunboat didn't show up by then, the trio would probably be caught.

They waited and waited. At the first light of dawn, Charley spotted a Union vessel. "Let's go!" he shouted. They hopped in a crude boat — a dugout made from a cypress log — that had been hidden in the brush. Pushing out from the shore, Charley said, "Good-bye to slave life forever!"

As they neared the Union gunship, a sailor shouted, "Who are you?"

"Friends of the Yankees," Charley replied. "We're runaways from the Felton plantation."

"Are your owners Union people?"

"No, they back the Confederacy."

"Come aboard." The jubilant runaways climbed onto the vessel and kissed the deck out of happiness. After they drank coffee and briefed the captain, they sat on the deck to soak up the warmth of the sun — and freedom.

But then they heard dogs barking and men shouting. "Sounds like we've been missed back at the plantation," said Joe, without a trace of alarm in his voice. Soon the pattie rollers appeared on the riverbank, shouting at the runaways.

"I'm tired of all that carrying on," said the captain. He ordered a gun loaded with a shell to be fired in the pattie rollers' direction. The shell burst in the air, sending the men and their dogs fleeing into the woods.

That night, the Union sailors went ashore, took Felton prisoner and brought him back to the boat. The next morning, the three runaways said hello to the shackled plantation owner. When he saw them, he cursed them and declared, "When the South wins this war, they will kill all the Negroes who ran away. I will make it my duty to personally kill all of you."

"The South can't possibly win, so I feel safe enough," said Joe.

"My, my how the tables have turned," Charley said to Felton. "Now I am free and you aren't."

When they reached the safety of New Bern, David and Joe chose to join a work detail that was strengthening the defenses on the perimeter of the town.

Charley asked to become a spy and was put under the command of Furney Bryant, an ex-slave like himself who escaped from his master's plantation early in the Civil War and now headed a group of black spies.

"Can you read and write?" Bryant asked him.

"Yes, and I can add and subtract. My master's son used to throw away his learning books when he was through with them, so I took them and taught myself."

"Splendid," beamed Bryant. "But what you are about to do can't be taught from books. It requires more than brains. It requires courage. Do you have courage?"

"I do. I'm willing to risk my life to end slavery."

"To ensure this freedom, you, as a spy, must go back into slave country."

"So be it," Charley said.

"Good. I need you to spy on the Confederate headquarters in Kinston. That's about forty-five miles from here — thirty of it behind enemy lines. Take a good look at the rebel encampments, make a careful note of their placements, and memorize the number of soldiers. Don't write anything down in case you are caught. Ask the Negroes you meet along the way what they know about the enemy, and bring this information back to me. But know that the rebels and the pattie rollers are just as likely to shoot you as look at you."

"Don't worry," said Charley. "I'll be careful. But first I need paper and a pen."

Charley then forged a pass saying he was a slave of a local plantation owner and had permission to travel. He made several other fake passes but left the name of the owner blank so he could fill it in later once he learned of a local plantation owner's real name from the slaves he would meet.

His first spy mission was a success. Getting food, rest, and directions from slaves, Charley spied on the rebel encampments in Kinston and returned safely to Bryant with a full verbal report. Armed with the information, Union troops led by Brigadier General John G. Foster left New Bern on a mission to destroy the Wilmington & Weldon railroad bridge at Goldsboro, a crucial link in the Confederate supply line. On their way, they battled the rebel forces of Brigadier General Nathan Evans near Kinston Bridge on December 14, 1862. The Confederates were outnumbered and withdrew north of the Neuse River. Foster then marched on with his men and, after a fierce battle in Goldsboro, managed to burn down the bridge.

Charley was sent to Kinston on another spy mission. But on the way back, two pattie rollers stopped him. He calmly showed them his pass, which had the forged signature of Benjamin Courtney, a plantation owner in nearby Dover. Charley had forged the name that he got from a slave a day earlier.

"That's strange," said one of the pattie rollers. "Ben is my cousin, and I know all his slaves. And you ain't one of 'em."

"I was lent to him by my master, John Marlow, over in Wise Forks," said Charley, trying hard to remain calm. He stared the man straight in the eye and hoped his lie was convincing.

"You keep walking on this road back to the Courtney plantation. I'll see you there later. Boy, you better not be lying. If I find out otherwise, I'll hunt you down like a dog and shoot you dead."

As soon as they left, Charley headed off into the woods. About two hours later, as dusk settled in, he reached a plantation and knocked on the door of a slave family.

"Are you the runaway the pattie rollers are looking for?" asked the father of the family.

"Yes, can you help hide me?"

"Not with those dogs. But I tell you what we can do." He led Charley to the barn and said, "Stick your feet in this bucket of turpentine. It'll destroy your scent and stop the hounds in their tracks." Charley did what he was told and then, with directions from the slave, fled into the night. The dogs did not follow him, and once again, Charley made it safely back to New Bern with important intelligence for the Union forces.

On his third mission, he was about five miles beyond Kinston with Willy Sampson, another teenage spy, when they were unexpectedly discovered by a rebel on horseback who had a pack of bloodhounds by his side. The young men fled into the thick woods, the dogs right on their tail. They reached a wide, swift stream and swam to the other side, climbed a large poplar tree, and rested. The dogs yelped and whined on the other side.

"We're safe," said Charley.

"But we're thirty miles from the nearest Union pickets," said Willy.

"They won't be looking for us anymore."

They jumped down and ran for hours and hours, taking short rest periods every 30 minutes, until they were within 12 miles of the Yankee lines. To their dismay, they once again heard barking dogs and men's voices urging on the hounds. Knowing that the dogs were after them, Charley and Willy sprinted into a swamp until they were neck deep.

"I don't know how to swim," Willy said.

"Neither do I," Charley said. "I wouldn't worry about drowning. If the dogs don't get us, the snakes probably will."

Somehow they managed to make it to the other side of the

swamp, but they were wet and cold. About two miles from the first Union pickets, the young spies were again being tracked by the hounds.

"I don't believe this!" Willy moaned.

"Not again! Willy, run for your life!"

As they made a mad dash for their freedom, they realized that their wet, soggy clothes were heavy and slowing them down. "The dogs are gaining on us!" Willy said.

"Strip down!" ordered Charley. While on the run, they threw off their coats, then their pants, and even their caps. The dogs were now nipping at their heels and the pattie rollers were only a few hundred yards away. "Keep running!"

Just as the dogs were about to take a bite out of the young spies, several gunshots erupted. The dogs screeched to a stop and the boys dived for cover. "Where are the shots coming from?" asked Willy.

Charley laughed. "It's coming from our side. Get up — get up and let's go." The Union pickets fired a few more shots over the heads of the young spies and forced the rebels to back off with their dogs.

Clad in nothing but their shirts, Charley and Willy stumbled across the lines and collapsed, safe in Union hands. After they got into new clothes, they gave their information to the general.

Now that the mission was complete, Charley went to Bryant and said, "I think I've done enough spying. I want to live to see another year."

Although no one knows what happened to Charley after he quit spying, Union military accounts praise him and other black men who gathered intelligence behind Confederate lines. They were known as the Black Dispatch, a name coined by General Rush Hawkins, the Union commander at Cape Hatteras, North Carolina. In 1864, he wrote of the black spies: "If I want to find out anything hereabouts I hunt up a Negro; and if he knows or can find out, I'm sure to get all I want."

The Boy Martyr

DAVID DODD, CONFEDERATE SPY
CIVIL WAR

1863–1864

The thought of being a spy for the Confederacy had never crossed David Dodd's mind. Sure, he despised the Yankees. He was distressed when they took control of his hometown of Little Rock, Arkansas, in September 1863. And he was upset that his family had been uprooted and forced to flee more than 100 miles south to Camden.

But a spy? The seed had been planted by Confederate General James F. Fagan, who was in charge of rebel troops in Camden. David had gone to the general's office and requested a pass so he could go to Little Rock to take care of some family business.

The general was acquainted with the Dodd family. David's father, Andrew, was a sutler — a traveling merchant who sold goods to the Confederate Army. David had helped his father, but then quit school after contracting malaria. He went to Monroe,

Louisiana, where he lived with relatives during his recovery. Once his health improved, he worked in the telegraph office there before joining his father, mother, and older sister in Camden.

"What's so important that you need to go across Union lines?" the general asked David.

"My dad has a plan to buy tobacco, which is becoming ever rarer because the Yankees keep destroying Southern fields," David replied. "He figures he'll store the tobacco and then sell it later when its value increases. But he needs to raise some cash because the more you buy, the better price you get, and so the more profit you make. He wants me to go up to Little Rock and talk to some investors."

"How old are you?" the general asked.

"I just turned seventeen, sir."

"I get it. The Yankees wouldn't be too keen seeing your father in Little Rock, but they won't give you a second thought. Any other reason why you're going up there?"

"Deliver letters to friends, family, and businessmen, sir."

Handing the teenager a permit that would let him pass the Confederate pickets, the general said, "There's no guarantee that you'll be allowed across the Union lines, but they'll probably let you." Lowering his voice, he added, "If they do, then upon your return here, I expect a full report on their military strength." He smiled and winked.

Is he serious? David wondered. *Or is he joking? Should I ask him? Better not. No matter how he answers, it'll be embarrassing for me and he might think that I'm really stupid. It's probably a joke — I think.*

"Thank you, sir," said David.

As he ushered the teenager out the door, General Fagan said, "Good luck on your trip. I hope it's a successful one. Make sure you see me when you return."

As he left the office, David thought, *Me, a spy? That's sort of ridiculous. My sole purpose on this trip is to convince those businessmen to invest in Dad's idea. But, wouldn't it be great to help the Confederacy? Well, maybe if I see something along the way . . .*

On a cold and blustery early December morning in 1863, David set out for Little Rock. When he reached Pine Bluff, he spent the night at the home of the Tomlinsons, who were family friends. When their seventeen-year-old son, Frank, was convinced that David hated the Union as much as he did, Frank told him, "I just returned from a spy mission to find military information for General John Marmaduke of Mississippi."

"You're a spy?" David asked.

"Not so loud," Frank said. "Even though we're in my house, there's no need to shout it out. You never know who might be listening."

"How do you become a spy?"

"By not acting like one," Frank replied. "Observe while you're pretending to do something else. Blend in. Make friends with the enemy. Don't ask too many questions or you'll arouse suspicion. Make people think you're just a kid who doesn't give a hoot who wins the war. If you write anything down, be sure to hide it on you so the Yankees can't find it."

Frank took off his boot and handed it to David and said, "Look at the heel."

David studied it and said, "I don't see anything." He gave it back.

Frank then twisted the heel until it swung to the side, revealing a hollowed-out area. "See? Here's where I keep my secret notes."

"Hoo-haw!" exclaimed David. "The Yankees would never suspect that you carved a hideaway in the heel of your boot."

"I like spying, it's exciting," said Frank. "I can help the Confederacy without going into battle. And if I get caught, what's the worst that can happen? They throw me in prison. They certainly aren't going to execute a kid."

The longer Frank talked, the more David's heart pumped with excitement. That night, he had made up his mind: *I'm going to be a spy!*

When David arrived in Little Rock, he moved in with his aunt, Mrs. Susan Dodd. The first thing he did was carve out a hollow space in the heel of his left boot. The knife he used was somewhat dull and it left several ugly gouges on the outside, but since his boots were getting worn out anyway, he didn't think it was a problem.

He spent much of the mornings meeting with businessmen and delivering letters — and observing the Union forces and their fortifications in the city.

But it wasn't all work. David also attended holiday parties and dances — lots of them — and quickly became popular with Little Rock's teenagers, especially the girls. They were attracted to the soft-spoken, handsome boy with the piercing dark eyes that matched the color of his slicked-back hair. Besides, there were few boys their age left in the area, except for some of the Union soldiers. And that gave David a clever idea. *I'll go down to the arsenal with a couple of girls and make friends with the young soldiers there*, he thought. His scheme worked to perfection. The girls loved the attention and the soldiers loved the flirting. And David casually asked questions — but not too many — about the Union's military activities in the city.

Meanwhile, he developed a special fondness for sixteen-year-old Mary Dodge, a cute and perky brunette. She was a strong supporter of the Southern cause, even though her father, R. L. Dodge, was a Vermont native on friendly terms with the Northern troops. In fact, Union officers were quartered in the Dodge home.

Confident that he could trust her, David escorted Mary to a holiday party and, in the middle of their waltz, revealed that he was a Confederate spy. She had hardly grasped the bombshell news when he whispered, "Help me spy on the Yankees."

She stopped dancing. "Why, David, whatever do you mean?"

He gracefully guided her back into the waltz and said, "You probably hear the Union officers talking in your home at all hours of the day and night. There must be times when they're discussing military strategy, troop movements, supplies, things like that. Tell me what they're saying."

"Well, I don't know. It sounds so dangerous. What if they catch me?"

"You're the sweet, innocent daughter of a Northerner. They would never suspect you of spying." The music stopped and he stared into her eyes. "If you believe in our cause — and I know you do — you'll help me."

She smiled and nodded. "For the Confederacy."

David saw Mary every day and jotted down in a small leather notepad the things she had overheard. He also gathered information by making friends with young Union soldiers, especially when he was accompanied by Mary Swindle and Minerva Cogburn, two local teenagers who had gone to dances with him.

When it was time to return to Camden, David was extremely pleased. *Won't General Fagan be surprised when he sees all this important intelligence I've collected,* he told himself. He had put the information into Morse code — a system of dots and dashes that represent letters and numbers — which he had learned while working in the telegraph office the previous year. Then he hid the notepad with the coded message in his hollowed-out boot heel.

On December 28, David obtained a pass from the Union granting him permission to cross Yankee lines into Confederate territory so he could rejoin his family in Camden. Riding a mule, he headed out of town, showing his pass to Union sentries at the city line. About eight miles out, David was stopped by another sentry. After David explained where he was going, the sentry tore up the pass, saying that the teen would no longer need it because he was entering Confederate territory.

An hour later, David reached the home of his uncle, Washington Dodd, and spent the night. The next morning, he resumed his trip south. But for some unknown reason, he took the wrong road — one that ended up back in Union territory.

It was a fatal mistake.

Not realizing he was now in an area controlled by the Union,

David was surprised when he encountered a group of Yankee cavalrymen. When challenged to see a pass or other identification, David explained that a Union sentry had ripped up his permit. They weren't convinced and ordered the teenager to ride his mule alongside them as they led him back to the outpost.

They're trying to harass me because they can, he told himself. Although he was seething inside, he kept a blank face and said nothing. His anger gave away to concern. *What if they search me? Could they find my notes?* The first hint of doubt crept in when he glanced down at his left boot. *I wish I had used a sharper knife on the heel.*

Because the sentry who tore up David's pass was no longer on duty and couldn't confirm his story, the soldiers took their captive to the nearby guardhouse where he was questioned by Lieutenant C. F. Stopral.

Just when things looked bleak for David, the sentry showed up to verify the teenager's story.

"Now can I go?" David asked the lieutenant, who was sitting behind a desk.

"Not so fast. Empty your pockets."

David pulled out Confederate and federal money and a Derringer, a small pistol. "For protection," he explained.

"I understand," said the officer. "What else?"

Maybe if I show him the letters, that'll satisfy him and he'll release me, David thought. From underneath his shirt in the back of his waist, the teenager removed several envelopes and gave them to Stopral. "They're from relatives and my father's business associates," said David.

Stopral examined the letters carefully to see if anything seemed suspicious or if sentences appeared to be written in a code. "They look innocent enough," he said. "I guess you can go."

The lieutenant got up from behind his desk. As he was returning the letters to David, one of them slipped from his hand and fluttered to the floor. Stopral bent down to pick it up when he glanced at the heel of David's left boot. He noticed it had been cut next to the sole and the edges were ragged.

"Boy, sit down and take off your boots."

A surge of panic jolted David. *He knows! Oh, my God, he knows!* Slowly David took them off and, with shaky hands, turned them over to Stopral.

The officer pushed and pulled on the heel of the left boot until it opened. "What do we have here?" He shook the boot until the tiny notepad tumbled out. "Well, well, well. It seems you've been hiding something from us, young David."

"It's nothing, really," said David, his mouth so dry from fear that it was hard to get the words out. "Just dates and names of girls. I had a lot of fun over the holidays."

Reading the penciled entries, Stopral said, "Looks like you've been a busy boy."

Then he reached the last two pages, which were filled with dots and dashes. "And what is this?"

David tried to clear his throat, but it felt like invisible hands were squeezing so hard he couldn't speak. Although it was freezing cold in the guardhouse, he suddenly was drenched in sweat. *It's all over. They got me. And there's nothing I can do about it.* He hung his head and remained silent.

"Looks like Morse code to me," said Stopral. Turning to one of the soldiers in the room, he ordered, "Get me the telegraph operator on duty, and make it snappy."

David didn't dare think about his fate. He did nothing but stare at his cold feet.

Minutes later, the telegraph operator appeared and deciphered the note. He wrote it down in words and numbers for the lieutenant to see: 3RD OHIO BATTERY HAS 4 GUNS — BRASS. 11TH OHIO BATTERY HAS 6 GUNS — BRASS. THREE BRIGADES OF CAVALRY IN A DIVISION. 3 REGIMENTS IN A BRIGADE, BRIGADE COMMANDED BY DAVIDSON. INFANTRY: 1ST BRIGADE HAS 3 REGIMENTS. 2ND BRIGADE HAS 3 REGIMENTS, 1 ON DETACHED SERVICE — 1 BATTERY, 4 PIECES PARROTT GUNS. BRIG. GENL. SOLOMAN COMMANDS A DIVISION, 2 BRIGADES IN A DIVISION; 3 REGIMENTS IN 1 BRIGADE, 2 IN THE OTHER. 2 BATTERIES IN THE DIVISION.

Stopral glared at David. "Boy, you're in a heap of trouble."

David was taken to a military prison in Little Rock, where Union officers vigorously questioned him for two days. They were extremely anxious to identify any Northern traitors or others who had given him detailed information about the Little Rock defenses.

Major General Frederick Steele, who was in charge of Union forces in Little Rock, believed a federal soldier had assisted David. The general promised to drop the charges if David would name the traitor. The teenager refused. "I'm not a snitch," he declared.

"You realize that the penalty for spying is death," one of the officers warned him.

They're lying, David thought. *They would never hang a kid. The worst that can happen to me is probably spending the rest*

of the war in prison. That's pretty bad but I can live with that.
I'm not going to spill the beans. I couldn't live with myself.

General Steele ordered a court martial, a military trial. On New Year's Eve — just three days after his arrest — the teenager faced a tribunal of six Union officers, presided over by Brigadier General John M. Thayer. Sitting between two defense attorneys who were called in at the last moment, David heard the formal charge against him:

"David O. Dodd, an inhabitant of the State of Arkansas, did as a spy of the so-called Confederate States of America enter within the lines of the Army of the United States, stationed at Little Rock, Arkansas, and did there secretly possess himself of information regarding the number, the kind, and position of the troops of said Army of the United States, their commanders, and other military information valuable to the enemy now at war with the United States, and having thus obtained said information did obtain a pass from the Provost Marshal General's office, and endeavor to reach the lines of the enemy — therewith; when he was arrested at the cavalry outposts of said Army — and did otherwise lurk, and act as a spy of the rebels now in arms against the United States."

"How do you plead?" General Thayer asked David.

"Not guilty, your honor," he replied.

With no time to prepare, his attorneys didn't put up much of a defense, not that David had one. He didn't even take the stand in his own defense.

"The law says that a spy is someone who, among other things, lurks and conceals himself or assumes a false identity in order to gather information," his lawyer William Fishback argued. "David Dodd has not done any of these things, so technically he's not a spy."

The court rejected that argument.

When the prosecutor showed the notepad, Fishback told the court, "The Morse code that David wrote was simply something he did to exercise his telegraphic skills."

First Lieutenant George O. Sokalski, assistant adjutant general of General Steele, then testified that the actual Union troop strength and weaponry was nearly an exact match of David's coded message.

In closing arguments, the prosecutor said, "David Dodd was caught red-handed attempting to enter Confederate territory carrying a coded message written in his own handwriting detailing all the military units under General Steele's command. There is no other word for it than spying."

The military tribunal didn't take long to reach a verdict. As David stood ramrod straight, he prepared for the worst — a conviction and lengthy prison sentence.

"The defendant is found guilty of spying for the Confederacy," announced General Thayer. "In accordance with military law, he is sentenced to be hanged."

Hanged? The word whirled around in his brain with the ferocity of a tornado until he couldn't see, hear, or think about anything but . . . *Hanged? No! No! This can't be!* David turned white and his knees buckled. He slumped in his chair. Turning to his lawyers, he bleated, "I'm just a kid. They wouldn't really hang me, would they?" When his lawyers cast their eyes downward, the awful, horrifying truth struck him so hard he couldn't breathe.

He was led back to prison to await his execution.

Over the next two days, Union officers urged David to tell them where and how he got his information, but he steadfastly refused. *I must remain loyal to the Confederacy,* he told himself. *I cannot go to my grave knowing that I betrayed Mary or the soldiers who helped me. No, I will go out as a rebel spy who didn't crack.*

Meanwhile, the Union's own investigation pointed to Mary Dodge as a suspected spy. David had visited her daily at her house, where Union officers were staying. When questioned by investigators, the officers realized they had discussed important matters, which Mary easily could have heard. Although General Steele was a tough, by-the-book military man, he couldn't bring himself to charge a sixteen-year-old girl with spying. He knew that if she were convicted, she too would face the gallows. Besides, her father was a Northern supporter. However, she had to be punished. So under personal orders from the general, armed guards escorted Mary and her father to a Union gunboat, which took them down the Arkansas River to the Mississippi. They were then transported to Vermont, where Mary was kept under house arrest until the end of the war.

While these plans were being made, people in Little Rock repeatedly appealed to General Steele to grant David clemency. "There is nothing I can do," said the general. "Death is mandatory under military law when a spy is convicted by court martial."

On the final night of his life, David penned a heart-wrenching farewell to his parents and sister. He wrote:

Military Prison
Little Rock Jan. 8
1 o'clock A.M. 1864
My Dear Parents and Sister:

I was arrested as a Spy and tried, and Sentenced to be hung today at 3 o'clock. The time is fast approaching but thank God I am prepared to die. I expect to meet you all in heaven. Do not weep for me for I will be better off in heaven. I will soon be out of this world of sorrow and trouble. I would like to see you all before I die, but let God's will be done, not ours. I pray to God to give you strength to bear your troubles while in this world. I hope God will receive you in heaven — there I will meet you. Mother, I know it will be hard for you to give up your only son, but you must remember it is God's will. Good-bye. God will give you strength to bear your troubles. I pray that we may meet in heaven. Good-bye, God will bless you all.

Your son and brother
David O. Dodd

David is believed to be the youngest spy hanged in the Civil War. In Little Rock, Arkansas, where he is considered a hero, an elementary school and street bear his name. Admirers hold an annual observance of his execution, complete with a 21-gun salute. Monuments honoring him dot the landscape, including one on the grounds of the Old State House. On David's grave in Mount Holly Cemetery in Little Rock, a marble scroll bears the inscription: BOY MARTYR OF THE CONFEDERACY.

The
Boy Scout

Joe Leysin stood at attention, his heart glowing with pride.

In front of him stepped the leader of his country, King Albert of war-weary Belgium. The king was holding a medal normally given to heroic soldiers and battle-tested generals, not teenage Boy Scouts like Joe.

As high-ranking members of the military looked on, the king pinned a military cross on Joe's chest. "I have the honor to decorate you with the Order of Leopold," the king said. "You are the youngest Belgian hero. I congratulate you and all the Boy Scouts who have done so much for their country."

"Thank you, Your Majesty," said Joe, still finding it hard to believe that a kid like him had, in the first year of World War I, turned into one of Belgium's greatest spy catchers.

The joy he felt at this great honor was tempered by a touch of sadness because the ceremony was taking place not in his native Belgium, but in the city of Le Havre in northern France. A year earlier, on August 4, 1914, Germany had invaded Belgium, triggering what was then called The Great War. The Germans quickly overran the outnumbered Belgian army, forcing King Albert to govern his nation from Le Havre. The war was fought mostly in a continuous line of trenches known as the Western Front. It stretched from the English Channel across southern Belgium and northern France all the way to Switzerland.

Before the war, when Joe was 15 years old and living in Brussels, Belgium, he joined the Boy Scouts, a newly formed organization founded by Sir Robert Baden-Powell, a British spy. The boy loved everything about the Scouts, especially the discipline, the outdoor activities, and the willingness to help others. But what really excited him was meeting Baden-Powell in Belgium and learning the basics of spying directly from the master. Baden-Powell was a member of the British Secret Service and had carried out spy missions in South Africa and throughout the Mediterranean. He wrote a military training manual for the Boy Scouts called *Aids to Scouting*, a book that included tips on how to spy on others. Joe read it over and over until he felt confident he would one day make a great spy.

But he also took a piece of advice from Baden-Powell to heart: "If you want to be a great spy, first try to catch a spy. That way you can learn what faults to avoid so you don't get caught."

When the war began, the Belgian Boy Scouts assisted military authorities by being guides, messengers, orderlies, assistants, and even sentries. Shortly after Joe became an assistant to

Captain Walter Van Brempt, it became clear that the teenager had an incredible knack for catching spies.

When an informant told Belgian authorities that two men dressed as priests were really German spies, Joe volunteered to follow them. Sporting an athletic build and a rugged face that made him look older than he really was, Joe disguised himself as a seminary student. He wore a Roman cassock (a long, black, long-sleeved garment) under a surplice (a loose-fitting, wide-sleeved, white gown), black dress slacks, black shoes, and socks. He carried a rosary (a string of beads Catholics use when praying) around his neck.

Seeing the priests at a café, he introduced himself and said he was a seminary student who was studying to become a priest. They appeared polite but made it known that they didn't want to strike up a lengthy conversation with him.

But Joe didn't care. "I don't recognize either of you," he said. "Are you new to the parish or are you passing through?"

"We are from Brussels on our way to Liege," said the younger one who identified himself as Father Henry.

"Oh, then you must know Monsignor Antoine. He's my uncle."

There was a slight hesitation as the two priests looked at each other. Then the older one, who called himself Father Bart, said, "The Catholic diocese is quite big. I don't believe I've had the pleasure of meeting your uncle. Now if you would please excuse us, Father Henry and I need to continue our private chat."

Joe bowed and walked away convinced that they were not who they said they were. He figured that if they really were priests from Brussels, they would have known that the name of the monsignor who Joe said was his uncle was really the bishop of the Brussels diocese. Every priest from that area would have known that.

Later that day, the priests were brought in for questioning, but they vigorously denied any involvement in espionage. "How dare you accuse two men of the cloth of such a crime," Father Henry protested. "I demand that we be set free immediately."

"In due time, Father Henry, if indeed you are a priest," said Captain Van Brempt.

Joe, who was still in his seminary clothes, walked in the room and startled the priests with his presence. He declared, "They aren't real priests, Captain."

Father Bart hissed, "And you are not a real seminary student. Apparently, you have chosen to ignore the commandment 'Thou shalt not bear false witness against thy neighbor.'"

Father Henry sneered at Joe and said, "You had better quit playing spy games and go run off and play soccer or some other diversion for boys your age instead of insulting two honest priests."

"I still think you are spies — and that you are carrying some secret plans," Joe declared.

"That's absurd!" thundered Father Bart.

Joe peppered them with religious questions on subjects that he had learned while attending Catholic high school, but they gave adequate answers. The two men were then thoroughly searched and their shoes and clothes were carefully inspected, but nothing was found on them.

"I'm afraid I must release them," Van Brempt told Joe. "I

have no evidence to keep them." Turning to the two priests, the captain said, "You're both free to go."

As the priests got up to leave, Father Henry looked at Joe and said, "I'm extremely angry at you, but I forgive you."

After they left, Joe said, "I know they're spies, Captain."

"Joe, you're young and inexperienced. You'll learn that sometimes there just isn't enough proof. And sometimes you're going to be wrong."

Joe slumped in a chair, shaking his head. *We checked their hair, the cuffs of their shirt and pants, the soles of their shoes, their belts, their socks. What did we miss?* From around his neck, he absentmindedly began fingering the beads of the rosary. *We examined their bodies for any diagrams that might have been drawn on their skin. Where could they be hiding those plans?* Then it hit him.

"Of course!" he shouted, leaping to his feet. "It's so obvious I don't know how we could have missed it. Captain, I know where they're hiding the plans!"

Joe charged out of the building, hopped on his bicycle, and pedaled around the town, trying to find the priests. He eventually tracked them down in the next village and called out, "Father Henry, Father Bart."

The men glared at him. "What do you want now?" muttered Father Henry.

Joe got off his bike, walked up to them and said, "I want to apologize to you. I was wrong. I meant no disrespect to you and certainly didn't want to question your faith."

"Fine, fine," said Father Bart grimly. "Now we must be going." He and Father Henry started walking away.

Joe stepped in front of them to block their path. Pointing to the rosaries that were draped around the men's necks, he said, "I couldn't help but admire your rosaries. Where did you get them?"

"At the cathedral when we were ordained," Father Bart answered. "Leave us alone. You've caused us enough grief and I don't . . ."

In a flash, Joe grabbed the rosary and yanked it off the priest's neck.

"What in God's name are you doing?" Father Bart stammered.

Joe then tossed it on the ground and stomped on it, expecting some of the beads to crack open. They did, but to his great disappointment there was nothing inside them. "I don't understand," he mumbled. "The plans had to be in there."

He looked up just in time to see a fist slam into his face. Joe hit the ground hard, but being a burly, strong teenager, he shook off the blow and scrambled to his feet. By now both men were running toward the woods so Joe gave chase. When the priests split up and headed in opposite directions, he pursued Father Henry and, with a flying leap, tackled him from behind.

Henry went down hard and Joe jumped on top of him and struck him in the jaw. Then he pulled the rosary off and broke open one of the beads. A tiny ball of paper tumbled out. "I knew it! I just knew it!" he shouted in triumph.

With the help of two soldiers who had been tailing Joe on orders from the captain, the fake priests were brought back to headquarters. The beads of Henry's rosary were broken open, revealing several more balls of paper. Each piece of paper contained the map coordinates of the French and Belgian military positions in the area.

"Joe," said Captain Van Brempt, "I'm sorry I doubted you."

The teen put his hand on the captain's shoulder, smiled, winked, and said, "You're forgiven."

A week later, a man and woman in their twenties were brought into headquarters after they were arrested on suspicion of being spies. They had been caught on a hill overlooking a fortress where they had been making drawings. During the arrest, officers seized the couple's artwork, art supplies, and picnic basket.

While Joe examined the items that the officers had seized, the captain began questioning the woman. Her boyfriend was put in a separate room where another officer grilled him.

"We were doing nothing wrong," insisted the woman. "We were trying to have a little picnic and I was making some drawings of my boyfriend, that's all. There's nothing secret about them as you can see."

The pictures, done in ink on a sketch pad, were simple but impressive portraits of her boyfriend. No matter how Joe and Van Brempt looked at the drawings, there was nothing to indicate they were anything other than portraits. A test of the paper failed to turn up evidence that a message had been written in invisible ink.

The couple told identical stories about who they were and where they came from. Both were thoroughly searched but nothing was found on them.

Van Brempt was frustrated and told his officers, "They match the description of two German spies who are supposed to be in the area, but unless we find some proof of espionage, we'll have to release them."

"Captain," said Joe, "this will seem crazy, but I have an idea." Then he whispered his plan.

Van Brempt rolled his eyes and shrugged. "Well, we've tried everything else, and nothing has worked so far. You're supposed to be the boy wonder, so let's give it a try."

They built a roaring blaze in the fireplace of the headquarters. On Van Brempt's orders, the young man took off his shirt and sat on a stool with his back facing the flames a few feet away. "This is an outrage!" the man shouted. Within minutes, he started to sweat and squirm. "You're going to burn me alive!" he yelled. "I'm innocent, I tell you. Innocent!"

"Relax, sir," said Joe. "A few more minutes and then we'll be able to see if you are telling the truth."

Finally, the man was allowed to stand up and move away from the fire. When he was told to turn his back to the officers, they stared in amazement. An elaborate butterfly drawn in dark blue had mysteriously appeared on the man's sweaty back.

"What is this?" asked Van Brempt.

"It's a tattoo, that's all," said the man. "A butterfly."

"I'm not sure I understand," Van Brempt said to Joe. "Can you explain?"

"Sure. When I saw the drawings she had made on her sketch pad of her boyfriend, he didn't have a shirt on. Then when I looked in her art kit, I saw a bottle marked with a liquid that you wouldn't use in art unless you were trying to conceal something. This liquid leaves no mark on the skin under normal conditions, but when exposed to considerable heat it shows up dark blue. I learned about it in science class. So I figured maybe she had drawn something on her boyfriend's back."

"So what?" said the young man. "There's no law against having a butterfly tattoo."

"Oh, I think it's more than a butterfly," Joe retorted. "Captain, one of the things I learned from Sir Robert Baden-Powell is that spies often will draw maps and diagrams inside another design. I'll bet if you study this man's back, you'll find that inside the butterfly are detailed plans of the fortress."

The woman put her hands to her face and moaned, "Hans, they got us. We can't talk our way out of this anymore."

"Quiet, woman!" the man barked. "Say no more!"

When officers examined the butterfly closely, they soon discovered that it did indeed represent a diagram of the fort. The number of guns, their sizes and positions were shown. Even the weak spots in the defense were made clear in the butterfly drawing.

"Chalk up another two spies for Joe," Van Brempt announced, slapping the teenager on the back.

Weeks later, Joe and the captain were sent to a village that Belgian forces had recaptured after Germans had invaded it. Artillery had destroyed much of the place, and now Belgian soldiers were taking up defensive positions.

"There has to be a spy here because the Germans seem to know exactly where we are going," the major in charge of the village told Van Brempt and the teenager. "They know every troop movement we make around here and they know exactly where to drop their bombs. We called you in because we need to find out how the Germans are getting their intelligence."

"Are any villagers still living here?" Joe asked.

"No one except an elderly woman," the major replied. "She had remained all through the German occupation, and had even managed to hide and stay behind when everyone else fled. She was in a cellar during our bombardment, and when we went into the town she came out to welcome us. She's a sweet lady and even does our laundry."

"Captain, I'd like to get closer to this woman," said Joe. "I'm going to put on some torn, dirty clothes and pretend to be a refugee looking for my family. Whenever you see me, act like you don't know me."

Later that day, dressed like a victim of war, Joe knocked on the door of the old lady. When she opened it, he said, "Please, I'm hungry and tired. Can you open your heart and home to me? I will help around your house to pay for room and board."

The frosty-haired woman's wrinkled face softened. Clutching the dark shawl that was wrapped around her head, she said, "Why, of course. I could use the help."

Her name was Hermoine Lablatt. She told Joe that even though most of the village had been destroyed and everyone was gone, she had refused to leave. "It was my home before the war and I managed to survive during the time the Germans were here. I see no reason why I should go now that the Belgians are in charge again."

For the next few days, Joe worked at fixing the damaged roof and rebuilding the crumbled stone wall that encircled the house. Meanwhile Hermoine was busy doing the soldiers' laundry. Every morning she would wash their clothes in a huge tub and then spread them on the ground to dry. Sometimes shirts and underwear hung on posts and sections of the stone wall.

Joe noticed that the friendly woman always came out to greet any troops who entered the village. He overheard her conversations, which seemed innocent enough, although she always managed to find out where they were going, where they came from, and how long they expected to be here.

He also noticed that when the conversations ended, she would return to the laundry that was lying out to dry and rearrange it. At some point during the day, a German plane would fly nearby, often drawing fire from the ground. Later, more German planes would arrive, this time dropping bombs on Belgian positions.

Joe was convinced that Hermoine was a spy and was using the laundry to signal German pilots where to drop their bombs. Pants were laid out in a straight line that pointed in the direction of the bombing target. The number of white shirts or underwear on the stone wall told the number of miles.

To confirm his suspicions, he arranged to have a soldier drop off some laundry and casually mention that his platoon of sharpshooters would be camping under an orchard northwest of town the next day. The lie worked to perfection. When the soldier left, Hermoine rearranged the laundry on the ground, and a short while later two planes dropped bombs at that exact spot where the platoon was supposed to be. Captain Van Brempt arrested her the next morning.

At first Hermoine denied everything, maintaining for days that she was innocent. But the German accuracy in bombarding the troops had ended with her arrest. She finally confessed, and said that she had agreed to spy for the Germans because they threatened to kill her. "They promised to spare my life if I helped them," she claimed. "I had no choice."

"Oh, you had a choice," Joe said. "You chose to be a spy on your own free will."

"Certainly not," she replied. "I love my country."

"That I believe. But your country is Germany, not Belgium." He reached into a bag and pulled out a pendant of the German leader Kaiser Wilhelm and held it up. "On the back of this is an inscription 'To Hermoine.' I found it in your dresser."

She hung her head in defeat. "Yes, I'm German," she admitted. "I had been purposely left behind to spy when the Germans retreated."

As Hermoine, who faced twelve years at hard labor, was led away, the major praised Joe, but admitted there was a serious problem with her capture. "It's good that you were clever enough to catch this spy," the major told Joe, "but it's bad because we just lost a terrific washerwoman."

Joe Leysin became a hero in Belgium during World War I because of his amazing success as a teenage spy catcher. He single-handedly unmasked more than a dozen German spies and helped capture many more. He inspired thousands of teenagers to join the Boy Scouts and serve their country in many non-combat ways such as spies, couriers, and orderlies. Sadly, two Belgian Scouts were executed by the Germans after being captured as spies. When Joe turned 20, he carried out several spy missions on his own. He often sneaked behind enemy lines and, using various disguises, uncovered secret war plans that were used against the Germans.

The
School Girl

MARGUERITE VOURC'H, FRENCH SPY
WORLD WAR II

1940–1945

The church bells bonged slowly and deliberately, the way they always rang when they signaled the death of a loved one in the village. Only this wasn't a funeral. It just felt like one for Marguerite Vourc'h and her fellow citizens of Plomodiern, France.

The bells tolled to let everyone know that the hated *Wehrmacht* — soldiers of Nazi Germany's army — had arrived. It was August 1940, less than two months after France had formally surrendered to the invaders. And now the day that everyone in Plomodiern had dreaded was here.

All at once, the small, picturesque seaside town that was perched so appealingly in Brittany, on the far western tip of France, had lost its charm. A crowd of somber-faced men and women, many in tears, lined the streets to watch two columns of soldiers march in perfect unison. Frowning, the slim, dark-haired,

14-year-old girl turned to her older sister, Elise, and hissed, "I hate the Nazis."

"Me, too," whispered Elise, 16, leery that a Nazi sympathizer might be eavesdropping. "We must do what Papa says — never cooperate with them."

"Oh, I intend to do more than that," declared Marguerite in a hushed voice. "A lot more."

She backed up her words with action by turning into a clever teenage spy.

Marguerite, her eight brothers and sisters, and her parents, Antoine and Margot, were one of the most respected families in town — and also secretly dedicated to defeating the Nazis. They had the resources. Antoine, a decorated World War I hero, was a wealthy doctor and councilman who owned two farms, a lobster boat, and, for fun, a speedboat. They lived in a stately three-story house surrounded by a colorful flower garden.

Three of Marguerite's brothers — Jean, Guy, and Henri — were in the French army and had not been heard from since France surrendered. She missed them all, especially Jean, who always lightened the mood at home with his silly magic tricks.

Shortly after the Germans' arrival in the village, a member of the Gestapo — the Nazis' secret police — inspected the Vourc'h house. He ordered the entire family into the living room and told them that an important colonel would be arriving within the month. "Monsieur and Madame, you have a beautiful house, one befitting the stature of the colonel. He will be using your bedroom as his sleeping quarters."

A wave of resentment swept over Marguerite. She felt so helpless because the family had no say in the matter. She wondered how the presence of the colonel would affect her father's work in setting up an underground resistance movement in the village. As the Gestapo officer got up to leave, he offered his hand to Margot. She refused. "I do not shake hands with Germans," she snapped.

Furious at the insult, the officer slapped her across the face with the back of his hand and then shoved her to the floor. "Mama!" cried Marguerite, rushing to her side.

In a rage, Antoine leaped on the officer's back and began punching him in the side of the head. The burly Nazi threw him off, whipped out his gun, and beat Antoine and Margot in the face before storming out the door.

Marguerite, Elise, and the shocked younger children tried to comfort their parents and tend to their wounds. A while later, Marguerite got a bucket of soapy water to clean the blood and scuff marks off the walls. "No, don't," commanded her father. "Leave the marks on the walls to remind us all of why we must fight the Nazis."

Marguerite clasped her hands in her father's and said, "Papa, let me help you in the resistance. The Germans don't pay any attention to me because I'm just a schoolgirl to them. But I can be valuable to you and the cause — as a courier and even as a spy."

"It's dangerous, *ma chérie*. They are ruthless. Just because you are a girl doesn't mean they won't torture or kill you if you are caught."

"I am not afraid. Please, Papa, let me help."

Antoine threw his arms around her and said, "I'm so proud of you, Marguerite."

Her first task was to help her father find volunteers for the resistance. It wasn't that easy because not everyone in Brittany was opposed to the Nazis. In fact, some of the French citizens helped the Germans and even spied for them. Other people were afraid to say anything against the Nazis.

When she visited her friends, Marguerite looked for signs indicating which side their parents supported. She peeked at the return addresses of their mail and noted the kinds of publications they were reading. She paid attention if they had extra rations or a new expensive purchase — clues that Nazis were rewarding them. She sometimes learned of their feelings by overhearing conversations and asking innocent questions, such as "What do you think the Germans will do to us?" or "Are all Nazis bad?" At the market and the park, she listened in on conversations, knowing that most adults talked freely in front of schoolgirls. When she identified a sympathizer of the resistance, she told her father who would then try to recruit the person.

Marguerite began bicycling out into the country, paying attention to where Nazis were setting up gun placements. Rather than write anything down, she memorized their locations and reported her findings to her father. Sometimes she took a pair of binoculars and scanned the coast, looking for German boats that were laying mines. With her, she kept a notebook full of notations about seabirds so that if the Nazis ever questioned her, she could support her lie that she was gathering information for a school report.

After one such spy mission, Marguerite bicycled home only to find an armed German soldier guarding the house. Once inside, she found her three younger sisters and baby brother huddled in a corner of the kitchen, holding on to each other.

"What's the matter?" she asked.

"The German colonel is here," said her nine-year-old sister, Simone. "He's going to be living with us and we're scared of him." Still fresh in their minds was the beating the Gestapo officer gave their parents.

"Let me see if he's all that frightening," Marguerite said. She walked up the stairs and met him at the top of the landing. He was a distinguished man with graying hair, a lit cigar in his mouth, and a monocle squeezed into his eye. In his crisp, neatly pressed uniform, he politely tipped his hat to her, but she gave him the cold shoulder and walked past him as if he wasn't even there.

After she returned to the kitchen, she told the kids, "You shouldn't be that afraid of him. He wears lifts in his shoes and a cap that's two inches higher than normal. You see, he's really a little man trying to make himself look bigger and more important than he is." The children giggled and wanted so greatly to believe he wasn't dangerous. But deep down they knew he was.

The Vourc'h family never talked to the colonel. They practiced *le silence de la mer* — the silence of the sea — a cold, hushed chill that made clear the contempt they felt toward this stranger. They went on with their lives, speaking in French — which he didn't understand — and ignoring his presence, walking past him as if he were a ghost.

Within months of the Nazi invasion, Antoine had built up a network of homegrown spies for the resistance. Marguerite's brothers Jean, Guy, and Henri had made it to England for training with M19, a division of the British Secret Service that was involved in escape and evasion of soldiers and airmen behind enemy lines.

Robert Alaterre, a young man who had trained with the Vourc'h brothers, met with the family at their home. He told them he had arrived with a small spy ring that was assigned to collect intelligence in the area and help return downed airmen to England. "I want to set up our radio in your house," Alaterre told Antoine. "I'll live here, pretending to be your nephew."

"But the colonel is living here," Antoine said. "In fact, he's upstairs as we speak."

"That's perfect," said Alaterre. "He'd never suspect any Frenchman so foolish as to actually transmit from this house." He laughed. "Imagine that. I will be guarded by the *Wehrmacht* and they won't even know it."

The radio was smuggled into one of the children's bedrooms on the first floor and hidden in a trunk. Whenever Alaterre transmitted from the room, the younger children played in the hallway and acted as a lookout. If any German came down the hall, the kids would alert Alaterre by throwing a rubber ball at the door.

"Aren't you afraid you will get caught?" Marguerite asked Alaterre.

"No. As long as I have a ten-second warning, I can hide the radio and jump out the window."

The next day, Marguerite hopped on her bicycle to get eggs from the family farm about five miles away. When she arrived, she noticed a metal tower, about the size of a cathedral spire, had been built in one of the fields.

"What on earth is that, Mademoiselle Seznec?" she asked the caretaker's wife.

"I overheard a soldier say it was to talk to the submarines," replied the woman.

German submarines, known as U-boats, were lurking off the coast and torpedoing British and merchant ships loaded with needed supplies and troops for France. Marguerite hurried home and told her father and Alaterre about the Nazi's transmission tower.

"British ships have been sitting ducks out there because of those U-boats," said Alaterre. "I will radio your information immediately to England."

Two days later Marguerite went back to the farm to collect more eggs. As she rounded a curve in the road, she noticed that the tower was gone. Where it once stood was now an enormous crater.

"Mademoiselle Seznec, what happened?" Marguerite asked.

"Oh, it was terrible, but in a good way," the woman replied. "I was hanging my wash when a British plane flew overhead and bombed the tower. I was thrown from my feet by the explosion even though it happened a half mile from here. But the tower is no more. And that is a good thing, no?"

"A very good thing, Mademoiselle."

Later, when Marguerite bounded into the house and gave Alaterre the news, he whispered, "How does it feel to be a spy, Mademoiselle Marguerite?"

"I want to scream for joy . . . but," she whispered, pointing to the colonel's room upstairs, "I will save it for another time."

A few days later, Marguerite was on the second floor when she saw the colonel walk down the stairs and head toward the back door rather than the front like he always did before. That meant he would go past the room where Alaterre was transmitting. Her little sister, Simone, was supposed to be on the lookout, but she had gone to the bathroom.

Seeing the colonel stop in front of the door and put his hand on the doorknob, Marguerite told herself, *Do something, anything! But do it now!*

She took a deep breath, screamed, and threw herself down the stairs, tumbling head over heels until she landed in a heap at the bottom. The colonel turned around and ran to her. She was bruised and her head hurt, but otherwise wasn't injured. However, she pretended to be in pain and moaned and cried, knowing her act would give Alaterre plenty of time to hide the radio. "Oh, I am so clumsy," Marguerite said. "I can't believe I tripped and fell down the stairs. I am better now." After the colonel helped her to her feet, he entered Alaterre's room and looked around until he was satisfied that there was nothing suspicious. Then he left through the front door.

Afraid that the house wasn't secure enough, Antoine convinced the local priest to let Alaterre transmit radio messages from the church. That evening, the priest came over for dinner. When he left, he carried the radio under his cape and was accompanied by Marguerite who had a basket of wires, a folded-up antenna, and other gear concealed under several loaves of bread. They hid the equipment under the altar.

About a year after the invasion, a ruggedly handsome, tanned man about 20 years old appeared at Marguerite's door. "My code name is Raoul," he said. "I was trained in England by M19 and sent by your brother Jean to join the resistance here."

Not having received any message about him from Jean, Marguerite was leery. "How do I know you're not a Nazi spy?"

Raoul reached behind the girl's ear and said, "Jean told me that you always hid a coin behind your ear." He drew his hand back, opened his palm, and revealed a penny that he had concealed in his hand the whole time. Few outside the family knew about Jean's love for magic. Marguerite laughed at Raoul's trick and invited him into the house. A coded message from Jean confirming Raoul's assignment came the next day.

Pretending to be her cousin, Raoul bicycled with Marguerite along the coast, gathering intelligence on German troops and battery placements and making sure British Army maps of the region were accurate. But he often disappeared for days at a time. When he returned, he said only, "I was on a mission." She never asked him what he did — the less she knew, the better. Besides, he seldom talked about himself or his undercover work.

Marguerite had a crush on him, although she tried not to show it. He had an easygoing manner, a good sense of humor, and was always considerate. She loved the days when they went cycling together so she could be with him. It also was a chance for her to share her feelings about life as a spy — something she couldn't do with her friends.

"I can't have real close friends," she confided to Raoul. "I can't say too much about the war for fear I might give myself away. I sometimes worry that when I am delivering a secret document or listening in on a conversation, I'll do something stupid."

"Whatever you do, you must do it with the utmost confidence," he said. "If you are scared, it can lead to a dangerous situation for you and the resistance. Fear will make you do the wrong thing. Your face will look different and you will smell different and you will do one little thing that doesn't seem normal for you. Gestapo officers are very good at recognizing this. They are trained to spot people sweating or nervously rubbing their ear or hunching over as though they have something to hide. Just go about your business, but with confidence, *ma chérie*, confidence."

One of Marguerite's jobs was to relay information gathered by Yvonne Le Roux, a charming, personable older woman who everyone called Tante (French for "aunt"). Marguerite would visit Tante's house on the ruse that she was taking piano lessons. But really, Tante was giving the girl vital intelligence about the movement of German ships in the area. "It is so easy to trick the harbormaster into giving me the information I want," Tante once told her. "I whisper a few sweet nothings in his ear and bake him a fruit tart, and I learn so many details from him."

Tante would hand Marguerite sheet music that was coded with the ships' routes, cargoes, and times of arrivals and departures. The girl would give the information to Alaterre so he could radio England for possible bombing runs.

Many planes were shot down, and the British needed its stranded airmen returned because training new flight crews was lengthy and costly. Those who were hiding out in France relied on the resistance's help to get back to England. As the war progressed, Marguerite helped these rescued fliers by putting them in French disguises and sneaking them past German officers. She also gathered basic supplies for them while Alaterre made arrangements for the aviators to escape on French lobster boats.

One evening, she and Raoul waited at the train station to escort six escaping airmen who were disguised as French workers returning from a job in Paris. Raoul had been in Paris with them a week earlier, getting them prepared. "I spent days teaching them how to act like Frenchmen," he said. "I dressed them properly right down to their shoes and socks. Even the best German won't know they're British." As the train pulled up, he said to Marguerite, "Just for fun, let's see if you can spot the fliers."

She identified all six.

"My goodness," he said stunned. "How could you tell?"

"Raoul, it's not the way they are dressed that gives them away. It's the way they walk. They aren't sure of themselves. Confidence, remember?"

The local resistance received word that ten downed British airmen would be making their way to Brittany soon, so a plan was developed to get them home. In a coded message broadcast on the BBC — Britain's national radio network — Raoul was told where he could collect the money to fund the operation.

But Raoul failed to meet Marguerite at the train station when the disguised fliers arrived. Not knowing which passengers were the downed airmen, she went up to the ones she guessed were British and whispered a code phrase, "*Pouvez-vous réparer mon toit?*" (Can you repair my roof?). She guessed right. Five went with her sister Elise to a safe house while Marguerite guided the rest to Yvonne Le Roux's home.

When the girl arrived, she found Yvonne weeping. "Tante, what's wrong?"

"There is no easy way to say this: Raoul is dead!"

Marguerite's heart sank and she slumped onto the couch. Eyes brimming with tears, she croaked, "No, it can't be. What happened?"

"He was shot by a double agent. But like the true hero he was, Raoul swallowed the latest coded message before he died."

Marguerite buried her head in her hands and wept. "He was so sweet. And I never even knew his real name."

"It's a lot to ask, but we must carry on," said Yvonne. "Raoul would have wanted us to. We need to help these fliers get back to England."

Raoul's death meant Marguerite had to find a place to hide and feed the men until they could escape in her father's lobster boat. She approached the local priest who agreed to keep them in the church basement. They stayed there for several days until it was safe for the resistance to put them on the boat, which was captained by her brother Henri.

When Marguerite returned home that day, she found her mother and Tante in the living room going over a new code. "The fliers are on their way to England," she announced. "What a relief. It was . . ."

The girl was interrupted by harsh pounding on the front door. She opened it, and was startled to see three members of the Gestapo. "Where is Madame Le Roux?" one of them demanded.

"Madame Le Roux?" Marguerite repeated loudly, hoping Tante could hear what was happening from the other room. "Well, I . . . uh . . ."

"We know she's in here. Now get out of our way!"

"No, wait, you're making a mistake. . . ."

Pushing her aside with such force that she slammed against the wall and fell to the floor, the officers barged into the living room. "Madame Le Roux, you are under arrest!"

"On what charge?"

"Spying."

They grabbed her by the arms and dragged her toward the door. As they passed the dazed girl, Marguerite knew Tante would be tortured and probably killed or at best sent to a concentration camp. Marguerite stared into Tante's eyes and saw fear — but also defiance, a silent message to keep fighting for the resistance.

But that wasn't the only big blow Marguerite received that night. She found a coded message from her father that read, GESTAPO LOOKING FOR ME. GONE IN HIDING.

Minutes after she burned the message, the Gestapo burst into the house and confronted Marguerite's mother. "Where is your husband, Madame Vourc'h?"

Margot broke down and wailed. "He left us! He deserted us, the coward! Oh, what are we going to do?" Tears gushed out of her as she put her head on the chest of one of the officers and sobbed.

"Madame, please, we need to find your husband."

"He's gone!" she cried. "He took off like a frightened dog

to who knows where. And now we're all alone to fend for ourselves!"

When the Gestapo left, Margot wiped away her tears and in a calm voice asked Marguerite, "So, how was my performance?"

"I had no idea you were such a great actress, Mama."

But then Margot's eyes welled up again. "It wasn't all acting. I'm so tired, Marguerite. I just want peace and for all of us to go back to our former happy lives."

"Every day brings brighter news about the war, Mama. The Germans are losing. It won't be long. You'll see."

"I'm sorry for seeming weak, *ma chérie*. The strain is getting to me."

"I've got a great idea, Mama. Come with me to Paris. I have to take some secret documents to an agent there. After I've done that, we'll do a little shopping to cheer you up. Elise can take care of the kids until we get back."

So mother and daughter went to Paris. Hidden in Marguerite's suitcase were folders bulging with military information. While handing over the secret documents, Marguerite was told by the agent, "We just heard from the BBC that your last group of fliers made it safely to England." He handed her the transcript of the coded broadcast: FRIENDS OF THE THIRD SON OF THE BRITTANY DOCTOR ARE ENJOYING BANGERS AND MASH.

Marguerite was relieved, but also concerned. The coded message seemed much too obvious. *How many doctors in Brittany have at least three sons?* she wondered.

On the day that she and her mother were planning to take the train back to Plomodiern, Alaterre showed up at their hotel room. "You can't go home," he warned. "The Germans figured out the coded BBC message. Elise told me that the Gestapo came into the house with their guns drawn, looking for you both. When she told them that you had deserted the family, just like her father, they refused to believe her at first. But she is a good actress and finally convinced them you'd never be back."

"But the resistance in Plomodiern . . ." said Marguerite.

"We're losing too many people," he said. "We believe there's a German spy in our midst so we need to find him before we can do any more undercover work. Elise and I will look after the kids. But if you value your life, and theirs, hide somewhere in Paris. Don't go home."

For the next three months, Marguerite and her mother holed up in a rundown Paris hotel, having barely enough money for food. Every footstep out in the hallway, every knock on the door brought fear that the Nazis had found them.

On August 25, 1944, Marguerite awoke to a rousing sound outside that kept growing louder. She peeked out the window and then announced, "Mama, Mama, they're here!"

Margot bolted up, panic-stricken. "The Nazis?"

"No, Mama. The Americans. Paris has been liberated!"

"Oh, thank God," Margot said, weeping. "The war will be over soon and we can go back to being a family again. No more hiding."

"And no more spying."

After the war, the family was reunited. Marguerite graduated from high school and was studying to be an architect when she fell in love with James Garden, a Scotsman who later became a surgeon. They married in 1948 and moved to Scotland where they raised seven children. In 2003, Marguerite was awarded the Légion d'Honneur, France's highest honor, for her heroism during World War II.

— The —
Peasant Girl

INGEBORG KLEIN, GERMAN-BORN FRENCH SPY
WORLD WAR II

1943–1944

Working undercover as a French peasant made teenage spy Ingeborg Klein tingle with excitement. To her, it was a role she was playing, like a serious actress on a Broadway stage. Only this drama was real and a poor performance could end in death — most likely hers.

Living on the edge in a tiny village in France at the height of World War II, the spunky girl spied on German soldiers, knowing that one false step, one slipup, could spell doom for her and those in the local resistance movement. But it was worth the risk because it gave her a chance to get even with the Nazis.

Every morning as she got ready for another day of spying, Ingeborg's mind flickered with images of how she ended up here in the village of Avy — and why she hated the Nazis. The mental pictures were starting to fade with the passage of time.

Still, Ingeborg was determined to remember all the details of what had happened to her over the past five years, the good and the bad.

The slide show in her brain always began the same way: Ingeborg living an idyllic life in a sprawling, beautiful house in Prussia, Germany... Playing board games with her sweet-natured mother, Marte, and kind-hearted father, Frank... Practicing the rituals and traditions of their Jewish faith.

But the snapshots soon turn ominous: Adolph Hitler, the leader of the Nazi Party, creating laws that stripped Jews of their rights... The Gestapo harassing Ingeborg's wealthy father for speaking out against Hitler... Nazis taking over the family's land holdings.

And next come the frightening images of that fateful night of November 9, 1938 — *Kristallnacht,* The Night of Broken Glass: Rampaging Nazi-backed mobs freely attacking Jews in the streets, in their homes, and at their places of work and worship... Invaders vandalizing and looting her home while she and her parents cowered in terror... Her father fleeing minutes before Gestapo officers charged into the house with guns drawn and a warrant for his arrest.

Then Ingeborg sees in her mind the most challenging year ever for her and her mother: Escaping the clutches of the Nazis and getting smuggled to safety in Belgium... Stowing away on a France-bound train that gets strafed by German fighter planes, killing nearly all in the next passenger car... Walking through France for the next five months, often stealing and begging for food, other times working on farms for something to eat and a place to sleep, usually a cold, smelly barn.

Finally, her mental pictures focus on the help she and her mother received from the French Underground: Providing them with new identities as French Catholics . . . Moving to Avy . . . Getting jobs and a room in the local hospital run by nuns.

When they settled in the village, Ingeborg, now 16, had no thought of becoming a spy. All she was concerned about was her own survival and that of her mother's. She worked as a nurse's aide while Marte helped prepare meals for the patients and staff. No one in Avy knew that Ingeborg and her mother were escaped German Jews. Their fake identity papers said they came from Alsace-Lorraine, a region along the French–German border. The town that they supposedly came from had been destroyed, so there was no way for the Nazis to check the records.

Also in their favor was their appearance. They both had reddish-blond hair, green eyes, and freckles — unlike many Jews who had dark hair, eyes, and complexion.

Ingeborg had an easier time than her mother becoming French and blending in with the villagers because she spoke the language. Marte didn't know French so she had to pretend she was a deaf mute. To further protect their true identities, they were careful in public not to speak German or act like they understood it.

Because German troops often came into the village, and some residents supported the Nazi cause, Ingeborg and her mother were wary of trusting anyone. Still, they were friendly and attended Catholic mass on Sunday like many of the villagers did.

"I heard they brought in another German defector," Marte

whispered to Ingeborg late one night in their tiny quarters at the hospital. "He was shot up pretty badly."

"Hush, Mama," said Ingeborg. "You know you aren't supposed to talk."

"I'm afraid if I don't exercise my voice, I will lose it for good. This silence is so frustrating."

"Well, I'll keep teaching you a little French every night so one day you can tell everyone in French that you recovered your voice."

There was a gentle knock on the door. "Ingeborg, it's Sister Therese. Are you awake? We need your assistance with the new patient."

"I'll be right there, Sister," said Ingeborg. Before opening the door, she turned to her mother and silently mouthed the words, "No more talking."

The patient was a German soldier who had deserted his unit. Even though the doctor took out three bullets from him, he was still writhing in pain and had a fever. He seemed quite agitated and kept mumbling, but because no one at the hospital spoke German, they couldn't understand him.

"Ingeborg, you have such a calming influence on patients," said Sister Therese. "Hold his hand and keep a cold washcloth on his forehead. We're not sure if he will make it through the night."

When she was sure no one else was around, Ingeborg whispered a few comforting words in German to him. He clutched her hand and with great effort murmured, "I'm . . . dying. . . . Please . . . get message to . . . wife."

Although Ingeborg knew it wasn't wise to risk blowing her

identity, her heart told her otherwise, and she found paper and pencil. She carefully jotted down the loving, final message dictated by the dying soldier. She promised to mail the letter to his wife.

The next day, after mass, Pierre Latrell, owner of a small inn and tavern, threw a little barbecue for hospital workers to thank them for taking care of his aged mother who had died several weeks earlier after a lengthy illness. During the get-together, he took Ingeborg aside and said in a soft voice, "I could really use your help."

"Certainly, monsieur. Do you need me to sweep the floors or help with the housekeeping?"

"No, something much more important. And very dangerous."

"What is it?"

"I understand you speak German."

Ingeborg shook her head, afraid that her cover was blown. "You are mistaken, monsieur."

"I doubt that Sister Therese would lie to me. She heard you talking with the German defector last night."

"But I — I . . ." She started to move away from him.

"Ingeborg, it's okay. She's against the Nazis just like you are."

"We shouldn't be talking like this. How do you know I'm not a Nazi supporter?"

"Because you are filled with compassion. And I've seen how you look at the Nazis with contempt." He glanced around to make sure no one else was listening. "Ingeborg, we want you to spy on the Nazis for the French Underground."

"But why me?"

"You speak French and German. And you're so petite and

skinny that you don't even look fourteen, so the Nazis are even less likely to suspect you are a spy."

Her mind was reeling. *Me, a spy? It sounds so crazy, so scary ... so ... so exciting!* Here was her chance for revenge. No longer would she feel like a victim of war. No longer would she feel so helpless while the Nazis steamrolled their way through Europe. Now she could do something useful for the resistance.

"Will you at least think about it?" he asked.

"There's nothing to think about, monsieur," she said. "When do I start?"

"*Fantastique!* You will work in my inn, waiting on tables and doing some housekeeping. You will be the ears of the resistance. Many German soldiers on leave pass through Avy and stay at my inn for two or three days. I suspect they talk very openly, especially after they've had a few beers. You're the only one in the village who understands German. The soldiers will never assume a young girl in a small village in the middle of France would know what they're saying."

The rest of the day, Ingeborg couldn't stop shaking. *I'm going to be a spy!* She knew the perils she faced if the Nazis found out, but she still looked forward to this new adventure, no matter how treacherous. *I can't tell Mama because she will think that it's too dangerous. She will do nothing but worry herself silly. No, she must not know.*

The next day, Ingeborg began cleaning tables, pretending to be a simple French peasant. She kept alert, listening for conversations that might prove helpful. Most often the soldiers talked about their families back home and what they wanted to do after they won the war and how much they admired Hitler.

She was annoyed later that day when a loudmouth German captain made belittling remarks about the villagers to two sergeants: "The people here are so dumb the swine in their fields have more brains." The sergeants roared with laughter. Then he cracked some tasteless jokes about Jews.

I wish I could throw this pitcher of beer in his face, thought Ingeborg, who didn't realize how difficult it was for her to go about her business acting like she didn't understand what the Germans were saying.

Ingeborg went upstairs to calm down. She was dusting in a room when, from the open window, she saw the obnoxious captain step outside directly below her. *There's that awful man.* She noticed a clay flowerpot on the windowsill in front of her. *Hmm, what would happen if I "accidentally" nudge this pot with my elbow like this . . . ?* She shoved it off the windowsill. The flowerpot landed directly on the officer's head and shattered, spilling dirt and flower petals over his uniform. The unexpected impact temporarily dazed him.

When the captain recovered, he looked up at the open window and ordered his sergeants, "Find out who did this! That person will pay with his life!"

They stomped up the stairs and into the room where they found Ingeborg innocently sweeping the floor. "Did you throw a flowerpot at Captain Deitrich?"

Ingeborg, pretending not to understand German, looked at them blankly. They grabbed her and dragged her downstairs and out the door to face the officer. "Did you do this?" he yelled at the girl in French.

"It was an accident," she pleaded. "I swear. I was sweeping the room and my broom hit the flowerpot. I didn't realize it had fallen on you until the sergeants came. I am so very, very sorry." She pretended to cry. "Please let me clean off your uniform." She started to brush it with her broom, but he angrily gripped it and flung it aside.

"You stupid nincompoop!" he shouted. "Get out of here before I feed you to the dogs!" Turning to his sergeants, he said, "See? This is what I mean by how stupid these people are here."

Ingeborg went back to work, feeling smug about her acting performance. It felt so good to get away with that little caper. But her glee was short-lived when Pierre stormed into the room, seething.

"Don't you *ever* do something so reckless like that again!" he thundered. Lowering his voice, he declared, "If you want to be a spy, then act like one . . . and that means you act invisible. Don't bring any attention to yourself. It's a good thing the officer was in a good mood or he would have shot you on the spot."

"I'm sorry."

"Sorry? There is no sorry in spying. Perhaps I overestimated you. Perhaps you are too young for this job. If I can't trust you to behave, then you are through as a spy. Do you understand?"

"It will never happen again. I promise." When Pierre left, she thought, *Maybe what I did was wrong, but I'm still glad I did it.*

Over the next year, while she cleaned tables and served food, Ingeborg continued to eavesdrop on the conversations of the German soldiers. She heard — and relayed — information about troop movements, the status of Allied bombing runs and even soldiers' thoughts on their generals' military strategy. She never gave any soldier a reason to suspect she understood them.

One day she overheard them talking about an American plane, a P-51 fighter, that had been shot down in a dogfight with two German planes. The pilot had ejected and was descending in his parachute while the other planes shot at him.

"We know he's injured, and hiding near here," said a sergeant to a table of privates. "I'm aware you're supposed to be on leave, but it's been canceled." He spread a map out onto the table. "We think he's somewhere in this two-square-mile area. We must search every farm until we find him."

Wanting to get a glimpse of the map, Ingeborg took a half-finished mug of beer, put it on a tray and then deliberately stumbled, causing the mug to spill and splash beer on the sergeant's sleeve.

"*Mon Dieu!* I am so sorry," she muttered in French. She used her rag to wipe the beer off the soldier.

"You incompetent wench!" he snarled. "Get away!" He slapped her across the face, sending her crashing into the table behind her and onto the floor. She scrambled to her feet and, pretending to burst into tears, hurried into the kitchen.

"What happened to you?" Pierre asked.

Dabbing her bloody lip, she told him about the downed flier. "I know where they are looking because I got a glimpse of their map," she said. "It's the area north of the bridge."

"I'll get someone over there right away," he said. "We have to find him before the Germans do."

Hours later, the French Resistance had rescued the injured pilot and moved him to a safe house. Ingeborg arrived with needed medical supplies to treat his bullet wounds, which fortunately weren't too severe. Soon Pierrre made arrangements for him to get to Spain and eventually back to his base in England.

Ingeborg carried out her spy duties without knowing who else was involved in the local underground. Pierre hinted that there were other teenage members of the resistance in the region, but he didn't want her to know who they were or what their jobs were. And he declined to tell them that she was a spy. It was safer that way. For all she knew, some of the teens were escaped Jews who had taken on new identities just like she had done.

Once, while waiting on a table of German soldiers, Ingeborg overheard them complaining that Allied planes had successfully bombed a vital railroad supply line.

"We're low on ammunition," complained one of the soldiers. "But another train with boxcars full of laborers is on the way. They'll arrive in Chalais tomorrow and then we'll put them in trucks to fix the rails. It should be ready within two or three days."

"Hush!" ordered the captain. "Don't talk like that in public, even if you are just whispering."

"But they're only French peasants here," the soldier said. "They don't know any German."

Ingeborg went into the kitchen to tell Pierre what she had heard, but he wasn't there. When she served the men their meals, the captain stared at her. After she set the plate down in front of him, he smiled at her and said in German to the others at the table, "If she takes another step, I will shoot her."

She hesitated for just a split second. *Don't stop!* Her veins ran cold with fear. *Just keep walking.* The terror she felt instantly dried her mouth. *He's testing me . . . I hope.* Afraid her hands would start to tremble, she put down the empty tray and began wiping the nearest table, humming a French tune.

The captain got up and walked over to her and smiled as he whispered in German in her ear, "I am going to set this inn on fire and lock the doors and kill all of you."

He can't be serious, can he? She returned his smile and bowed. "More wine?" she asked in French.

The captain turned to the others and said, "You're right. She doesn't know German."

Ingeborg casually headed into the kitchen. Her close call had left her so scared that she hurried out the back door and threw up.

Pierre arrived moments later. "Are you sick?" he asked.

"I had to take a big test, but I think I passed. Pierre, the Germans are sending another train with workers to fix the bombed-out railroad tracks. They'll be arriving in Chalais tomorrow."

"I'll pass it on."

Thanks to Ingeborg's information, the second train was attacked by Allied planes and failed to get to Chalais. The supply line remained cut for the Germans.

That wasn't the only time Ingeborg had to wriggle out of a situation while pretending not to understand German. One evening, while she was working at the hospital, she had to provide towels for four soldiers who came to take showers there. It was common for troops to shower at the hospital. The four were caked in mud and smelled as though they hadn't washed in days. One of them pointed to Ingeborg and remarked to the others in German, "She is a pretty one. I think I will kiss her."

The thought of that stinking soldier touching her sent a shudder down her spine. But she kept her cool. Hiding a bar of soap in the towels that she was carrying for them, she spun on her heels and said in French, "Oh, no, I forgot the soap." She hustled out of the hallway and got another bar of soap and returned with the Mother Superior, the head nun, by her side. The girl gave the soldiers soap and towels, but the sergeant did not approach her. As she and the nun walked away, Ingeborg heard him say to the others, "She's a good-looking kid. Too bad she's here with all these old nuns."

Days later, Pierre asked Ingeborg, "I need you to deliver a map to one of our people within the hour. You can't afford to be late."

"I'm at your service, monsieur."

It wasn't as easy as it sounded. Two weeks earlier, the Germans ordered every villager to the town square. Then the Nazis announced they had caught a courier trying to smuggle parts for bombs to the resistance. They led a bound young man, Louis St. Jean, the local bread maker, to the steps of the town hall. And there, in front of the villagers, he was executed. "Let this be a lesson to the rest of you," said the colonel in charge.

Ever since, the German soldiers had set up checkpoints at different times and places and conducted random searches of adults only.

"They're not bothering the children," Pierre told Ingeborg. "The person you will meet is staying at a farm about two miles from here. You can take my bicycle. If you are asked where you're going, say that you're picking up some sausages from a farmer for the inn. You shouldn't have any problems getting through the checkpoint. Now hurry." He handed her a map printed on a silk handkerchief.

Unfortunately for Ingeborg, she reached a checkpoint where the soldiers were searching everyone — even children — and a long line had formed. It would take an hour just to get through.

"This is ridiculous," one of the German soldiers said to another one within earshot of Ingeborg. "Searching children. What are they supposed to be carrying? Secret chocolate?"

She couldn't turn her bike around without raising suspicion, so she took a deep breath and gave what she hoped would be a convincing performance. Going up to a French-speaking guard, Ingeborg cried, "Oh, please, sir, I need to get to my mother. She's sick in the hospital. I must get through now!"

The guard snapped, "Wait your turn!"

Ingeborg wailed even harder. "I need to see her now. She's very ill!" *Don't quit this act*, she told herself. *You might as well keep it up and hope for the best.* She kept sobbing and pleading.

"That crying brat is getting on my nerves," muttered the captain in German. "I don't want to hear her caterwauling. It's irritating. Just let her go through."

"Should we search her, captain?"

"No, get her out of here!"

The French-speaking German guard signaled for Ingeborg to go to the front of the line and told her, "Now quit your crying and move on before I change my mind."

"*Merci, merci.*" She pedaled on her bike and headed toward the hospital. When she was out of sight, she turned and took the long way to the farm where she delivered the map just minutes before the resistance fighter was scheduled to leave.

Like millions of others, Ingeborg and her mother rejoiced when the war ended in 1945. But their happiness was doused when they received word that her father, Frank, had been captured by the Nazis a year earlier and had died in a concentration camp. Having little reason to return to their home in Germany, they remained in Avy where Marte "miraculously" recovered her voice and her hearing. By then, she had lived there long enough to speak and understand limited French.

Ingeborg and other members of the local resistance were awarded medals from France's new president, Charles de Gaulle, the country's most famous general during the war. He had embarked on a tour of villages to personally thank members of the underground.

When President de Gaulle pinned a medal on Ingeborg, he gave her a kiss on both cheeks, and asked, "How did a young girl like you become such a good spy?"

"Acting, Monsieur *Le Président*," she replied. "Really good acting."

Ingeborg eventually immigrated to America and settled in New Jersey where she married and raised a family. She has given talks at schools about the Jewish experience in World War II and has also written for French publications. The French Underground is credited with the safe return of hundreds of downed pilots; the sabotage of countless Nazi transports, factories, and bridges; and its valuable assistance to Allied forces to liberate France.

The Hungry Orphan

CHOON KYUNG KO, SPY FOR U.S. MILITARY
KOREAN WAR

1950–1951

Aiming his rifle at the scrawny boy in the ragged clothes, the soldier growled, "Who are you and what do you want?"

"My name is Choon Kyung Ko," the boy replied. "My parents were killed last month when our village was under attack. I'm hungry and tired and I have no place to go. Please, can you help me?" Tears streaked down his dirty face. "I haven't eaten in two days. Please?"

The soldier put down the rifle and mumbled, "Go to that tent over there. They'll give you some rice and dried fish."

"Thank you, and many blessings to you," said Choon, wiping his wet nose and cheeks with the back of his hand. He bowed several times and then hustled to the tent.

Choon didn't really suffer from hunger pains and wasn't wandering aimlessly. It was all a trick to get into the fort of the enemy — a battalion of the North Korean army. The 14-year-old boy had conned his way inside to carry out a dangerous mission as a spy for the United States military.

It was September 1950, the early days of the Korean War. The communist-led North Koreans had attacked South Korea, crushing most everything and everyone in their path. Rushing to aid the poorly trained and ill-equipped South Koreans, the United States military, with assistance from the United Nations, leaped into the conflict with ground, naval, and air power. The fighting was fierce, and more troops were still needed to drive out the North Koreans.

By pretending to be a hungry, lost orphan, Choon planned to hang around the North Korean military installation and gather information for the Americans. The fort was one of several perched on the small islands that protected the harbor of the South Korean city of Inchon.

As he dug into a bowl of rice, the boy struck up a conversation with some of the soldiers and told a made-up story of how he was orphaned. Every so often, he would ask an innocent question: How long have you been in the army? Where do you come from? Do you have a family? Once he gained their friendship, he knew they were primed to reveal more worthwhile information. After all, who would think a skinny orphan was really a spy?

"Gee, I bet there are more than two hundred soldiers on this island," Choon said.

The soldiers laughed. "We have five times that many here," said one of them.

"And when you include all the other troops on these islands, there are more than four thousand," added another.

Pointing to a bunker, Choon asked, "What is that for?"

"For machine guns," the soldier answered. "We have bunkers all over. But they're not ready yet. We still have to bring more weapons in and secure them. Come back in a couple of weeks. Maybe then we'll let you shoot one for fun."

By the end of the day, Choon had learned plenty, including that the North Koreans had yet to set up their full defenses, were short of weapons, and were getting ready to mine the harbor. He committed everything to memory rather than write it down. He knew that if he were caught with any evidence that linked him to espionage or to the Americans, he would be executed on the spot. It made no difference to the vicious enemy how young he was.

Choon slipped away and hopped onto a sampan, a flat-bottomed boat, that took him to another island where he met with South Korean secret agent Kim Nam Sun, who was working for the U.S. Navy. After hearing the intelligence that Choon had uncovered, Kim told him, "This information will be a big help. Now go find a safe place and lay low for a few days."

"Why?"

"You'll find out soon enough."

At dawn on September 15, Choon was sleeping on a mat at a friend's house when he was jarred awake by a thunderous light show. He bolted outside where the sky flashed and the ground shuddered in a crescendo of exploding bombs, rockets, and shells.

An American invasion! Choon thought. *So this is what Kim was talking about.* The boy looked on in wonder at the awesome firepower unleashed on the shocked North Koreans. As screaming planes strafed the islands, more than 300 ships, boats, and landing craft unloaded an assault force of 70,000 troops who completely overwhelmed an enemy that was totally unprepared for the surprise attack. *It feels good, real good, knowing I did my part*, Choon told himself. *I can't wait to do more spying.*

The commotion from nearby machine-gunfire, overhead dogfights, and whining artillery soon faded away, but only in his mind. From deep within his consciousness, he now heard only the barking of his beloved dog, a mutt named Jin-ho.

Besides his parents — his father was a Christian missionary and his mother a teacher — Choon's greatest love was Jin-ho. The mostly black dog had a white patch on his side shaped somewhat like Korea. Smart and fun-loving, the canine could actually smile. He always brought joy to Choon whose early childhood was darkened by World War II when Korea was controlled by a brutal Japanese government.

From first to third grade, Choon was escorted by Jin-ho to and from school every day in his hometown near Seoul, South Korea. But then one day the dog didn't show up. The worried boy searched the neighborhood without any luck. What he did find alarmed him greatly — Japanese soldiers were rounding up all the dogs for reasons he didn't understand. "Don't worry," said his father. "Jin-ho is so smart he probably is hiding from them. He'll be back soon."

Choon chose to believe that his dog was okay and holed up somewhere. But a few days later, the eight-year-old boy was walking along the riverbank when he came upon a sight that made him sick to his stomach. Dog pelts — hundreds of them — were on bamboo poles drying in the sun.

Trembling from a thought that he didn't want to face, he asked a soldier, "What is all this?"

"Dog fur," the soldier replied. "We're going to turn the pelts into coats and gloves for the Japanese army."

Choon walked slowly down each row, an almost unbearable task, but one he forced himself to do. He had to know. Halfway down the fourth row, he spotted a black pelt with a white spot shaped like Korea. He was too shocked to weep.

That night, Choon took his father's straight-edged razor, sneaked out of the house, ran to the riverbank and, through tears of grief and rage, slashed every single pelt until they were all useless.

The next day, outraged Japanese officials put up wanted posters, offering a reward for the capture of the culprit. A witness had seen a skinny boy about eight years old running from the riverbank, so soldiers were going door to door, questioning children.

Afraid he would be caught, Choon confessed to his father.

"You can't stay here, Choon," his dad said. "Who knows how severe they will punish you — and probably me and your mother. I have to think of something."

Choon was sent off to Song-kwan, a remote mountain village 200 miles away in North Korea where his parents had built a church and school for the local peasants. A family there raised him over the next two years until the end of World War II in 1945 when Japan was forced to give up control of all of Korea.

Choon returned to his home and parents, thinking that life

could only get better. It did for a while. He enjoyed school and learning English from passing American missionaries who often spent the night with the family. The more English he knew, the more he dreamed of one day going to America.

But his hopes were battered in June 1950 when the North Korean army invaded South Korea, slaughtering thousands of innocent civilians, especially doctors, lawyers, missionaries, and teachers — and his parents.

Devastated and alone at 14, Choon moved in with friends for comfort and shelter. Hoping to channel the anguish over his parents' deaths and his hatred of the North Koreans into something constructive, Choon joined the Student Volunteers Army. It was an anticommunist group of 300 teenage spies headed by a South Korean officer with close ties to the U.S. military. After two weeks of intensive training, the kids were sent into territory held by North Korea to gather intelligence by chatting with soldiers and observing troop movements and buildups. The spy kids were told to give any intelligence they had collected to runners — specially trained young people who relayed the information directly to military officials.

Choon's first assignment was finding out the enemy troop strength on an island fort outside the harbor of Inchon. With the information that he and other spies provided to the U.S. military, the surprise attack was carried out with swift precision, allowing the American invaders to recapture Seoul.

Thrilled by the success of his first undercover mission, Choon went deeper into North Korea to spy. Thanks to the accent he had developed when he lived there earlier, Choon made a convincing North Korean.

He joined fellow spy kid Kwan Park, 15, in a village where Kwan lived with his anticommunist parents. The boys visited a temporary base camp of communist soldiers and made friends with them by running errands. After gaining the soldiers' trust, Choon and Kwan were allowed to go inside one of the army's new tanks. While chatting with the soldiers, the boys learned the number of tanks the unit had and where they were headed.

When the young spies left the camp for the day, Kwan boasted to Choon, "It's a lot easier than I thought to get those dumb soldiers to talk. They're too stupid to ever suspect kids like us of spying on them."

Back in the village, they noticed people gathering in front of the square. When the boys weaved their way to the front of the crowd, they saw several couples tied back-to-back with rope. Kwan squeezed Choon's arm and whispered with alarm, "The man and woman on the end are my parents!"

Speaking through a megaphone, a North Korean officer announced, "We have reason to believe that children in this community are acting as spies for the enemy. Here before you are the parents of the children we want to question. These children must submit to authorities immediately. If they are innocent, they have nothing to fear. But if they don't step forward by the end of the day, we will have no choice but to kill their loved ones."

Breaking out in a cold sweat, Kwan told Choon, "I have to go."

Choon grabbed Kwan's wrist. "Don't do it. They'll torture you and then kill you and your parents."

"I couldn't live with myself if I run away, knowing that I was responsible for my parents' death. I'd rather die than have that on my conscience."

"Your parents are going to be executed no matter what. Don't die, too."

"I think I can fake those communist goons into believing I'm a harmless village kid and not a spy. They won't get anything out of me."

Kwan shook off Choon's grip and stepped forward and shouted out, "Here I am. I'm Kwan Park. I'll answer your questions."

It was little comfort to Choon that he wouldn't ever face Kwan's dilemma. Choon had no parents anymore. But he was worried that Kwan would cave in and reveal that Choon was a spy, too. *I can't stay around here any longer,* thought Choon. *It's only a matter of time before they find out about me.* He headed in a southerly direction, hoping he would run into friendly forces.

Two hours later, an American soldier popped out of the bushes, aimed his rifle at Choon and said, "Halt, or I'll shoot!"

Choon had heard that young American soldiers were trigger-happy, shooting first and asking questions later. So in his best English, he responded, "I am a South Korean. I have important information for your commander."

"What is the password of the day?" the G.I. asked.

"How would I know? Please, let me see your commander. I'm on your side. You can search me and blindfold me if you want."

After being searched, Choon was led at gunpoint to a major who listened intently to Choon's report about the tanks. When two other spies confirmed the intelligence later that day, the boy was allowed to use the American camp as his base to spy on the enemy in other nearby villages. This time, whenever he returned to the base, he knew the day's password — usually something like "Yankee Stadium," or "Marilyn Monroe" (a famous movie star at the time), or "Cherokee Indians."

One day, the major called Choon into the tent and said, "I have some bad news about your friend Kwan. He and his parents . . ." He shook his head, his eyes downcast. "Choon, I'm sorry."

Tears didn't flow like Choon had expected. Instead, he felt his heart harden with bitterness. Revenge had trumped sorrow, and now he was even more determined to spy on the North Koreans. *I'm going to do everything I can to help the GIs defeat them. And I'm going to work alone.*

Wearing a typical black school uniform and black cap, Choon left the base for good. Because he was supposed to be a wandering orphan, he carried no possessions, not even a toothbrush or any identification. He traveled on foot for several days, sleeping in barns and in covered pits where farmers stored their vegetables. The weather had turned cold, and snow had started to fall in the mountainous region. In village after village, Choon would tell North Korean soldiers his tale of woe in a performance enhanced with sobs and a perfect regional accent: "I'm all alone. My parents are dead. I'm trying to get to my aunt's house but it's fifty miles away. I haven't eaten in two days and I'm very hungry and cold. Can I stay here for just a little while and get something to eat, please?"

It worked every time — except for some reason, he couldn't

140

cry in front of female soldiers. Even in time of war, his pride simply wouldn't let him do it.

Outside a mountain village near a large lake known as the Chosin Reservoir, Choon came across several battalions of soldiers in uniforms and hats he had never seen before. There was something different about them, even the way they spoke and looked. Next to them was an encampment of North Koreans. Once again, he played the hungry orphan routine, and once again it worked to perfection.

When he asked about the unusual troops he saw, a soldier told him, "Those are Chinese divisions. They are going to help us crush the Americans. The U.S. Marines are moving toward the reservoir and we will trap them. There will be no escape. It might be freezing cold but it will soon get very hot."

"There must be thousands and thousands of Marines," said Choon. "How can you be so sure you can win?"

"Because there are more than 120,000 Chinese waiting in ambush — ten times more than the Marines. The Americans are about to face their doom!"

Choon didn't know exactly where the Marines were, just that he had to find them immediately. As he started to leave the camp, he was stopped by a guard who ordered, "Come with me."

Taken to the tent of a captain, Choon gave his sob story, but to his dismay, the officer wasn't buying it. "There are no villages nearby and there's no reason for you to be here," sneered the captain. "You must be a spy."

"No, I'm not. My father lived near here and now he's dead." Choon wailed and dropped to his knees. "I have no one."

"Good. Then no one will miss you."

"I'm just an orphan. I'm willing to work for you for one bowl of rice a day."

"I can't afford to take a chance." Turning to the guard, the captain said, "Kill him."

"Come on, let's go," ordered the guard.

As Choon was pushed outside, he turned to the guard and said, "Please don't kill me."

"Shut up. Keep walking and don't look back."

The wind howled but all Choon could hear was the rapid pounding of his heart. *I hope the bullets will kill me quickly.* He began to pray.

"Start running . . . and don't stop. Understand?" said the guard. "Now run, boy, run!" Choon sprinted through the snow and ice, wondering with each step, if it would be his last. One shot, then another and another rang out. But from the sound, the bullets appeared to whiz far over his head. Seconds later, he dashed behind a huge boulder. Catching his breath, he turned around and saw the soldier was heading back to camp.

He couldn't kill me. He believed my story! Oh, thank you, God, thank you! Choon slumped to the icy ground and started to cry. But it was too cold for tears to fall.

In bone-numbing, below-zero temperatures, he worked his way down the side of a mountain until he was confronted by an American sentry, who, at gunpoint, brought the boy into a U.S. Marine camp.

After Choon told intelligence officers what he had heard, they refused to believe him at first. "We're at war with the North Koreans, not the Chinese," said a lieutenant.

"I saw them with my own eyes — thousands of them, many divisions," claimed Choon, describing the uniforms in detail. Other spies soon confirmed Choon's report.

At the time, three Marine regiments were strung out along 80 miles of a narrow dirt road that snaked its way up the sweeping slopes of the Chosin Reservoir. Just as Choon had warned, tens of thousands of Chinese soldiers soon emerged from hiding and pounced on the Marines, completely surrounding them. For the next five days, the greatly outnumbered Americans fought valiantly against the Chinese and the bitterly cold weather, finally breaking free for an epic escape down the frozen mountain trail.

Believing he would be less safe with the retreating Marines, Choon headed off on his own. Even though it was the dead of winter, he began walking back toward Seoul, 350 miles away. He figured it would take him a month. Trudging from village to village in North Korea and begging for food, he managed to survive — barely.

At one house, he met an elderly couple who shared a meal with him that was quite meager because they had so little themselves. They didn't believe his story that he was from a nearby village. However, when he learned they were anticommunists, he told them the truth — at least the part about trying to return to South Korea.

"You can help us solve a problem," said the woman. "We are hiding two wounded GIs. If the communists find out, they'll kill us and the GIs. You must take them with you to the American lines. It's about a hundred-mile journey."

"I can barely take care of myself," Choon said. "How am I going to take care of two Americans, especially when they're hurt?"

"You have no choice."

She showed him to the cellar where the men were hiding. They introduced themselves as Al and Harry, both in their twenties, both from New York City. They told Choon that during the retreat from the Chosin Reservoir, they both had been shot in the leg. In the confusion, they became lost but managed to avoid getting captured. Now they were weak, scared, and hungry. "You're our only hope," Al told Choon.

The boy knew he couldn't abandon them.

Because there was no way to disguise them — they were both about six feet, much taller than most Koreans — Choon decided that the three of them would hike only at night and hide during the day. It was slow going because the soldiers limped badly and their wounds were infected.

Each day while the two soldiers hid, Choon was out begging for food. What little he was given, which was hardly enough for himself, he shared with the GIs.

To pass the time as they plodded along during each teeth-chattering night, Choon peppered them with questions about life in New York. He loved hearing them talk about a city that never sleeps; a bustling world unto itself where neighborhoods like Chinatown and Little Italy thrive as their own mini-nations; where tall buildings tickle the sky and subways whisk people uptown; where millions cheer on the Dodgers, Giants, and Yankees and give standing ovations to the Rockettes at Radio City Music Hall and to famous stars on Broadway.

Talking about home seemed to perk up Al and Harry and fueled Choon's dream of one day seeing America's greatest metropolis for himself. But during the long bouts when they were silent, the pain from their wounds and the pangs from their hunger grew stronger. And the GIs grew weaker.

A week into their trek, they reached an abandoned farm near railroad tracks outside the city of Pongkang. Choon found an empty four-foot-deep vegetable storage pit — an excellent place to spend the day because it was covered with rice straw and protected them from the merciless wind. They huddled together to stay warm. By now the GIs were in bad shape, struggling to stay conscious.

As night approached, a freight train stopped about two hundred yards away from them. A North Korean soldier opened the door to one of the boxcars, revealing pallets of cans.

"Those are C-rations!" Choon exclaimed, almost drooling at the sight of the large supply of canned food that had been meant for American soldiers.

The two G.I.s moaned, "Food . . . food."

"The Marines must have left the C-rations behind during the retreat," said Choon. "Either that or the cans were stolen. I'll try to get some of those cans for us."

He sneaked across the field to the freight car and slipped inside. Then he stuffed the inside of his jacket with the cans, not knowing what they contained because he couldn't read the labels.

Scampering back toward the pit, Choon heard a guard shout at him, which was followed by a burst of gunfire. Snow kicked up on his left and right. Suddenly, he felt a sharp jolt in his foot, causing him to loose his balance. He fell, slamming his head hard against the frozen ground. Just before he passed out, he heard the guard yell, "I got him! I got him!"

A few minutes later, Choon regained consciousness. *Am I shot?* he wondered. *I don't feel hurt except for my head.* Still dazed, he remained sprawled on the ground and looked back to see if the guard was coming after him. *I don't see him. He's probably in his warm shack, thinking he killed me.*

Choon checked over his body for bullet wounds and discovered he had been shot — but only in the heel of his left shoe. Fortunately, the bullet hadn't penetrated his skin. *This is my lucky day.*

Afraid he might be detected if he ran, Choon crawled toward the pit. *Won't the GIs be happy when they see what I've brought them?* Outside the pit, Choon whispered loudly, "Harry, Al, it's me. I've got food."

There was no response. He crawled the remaining few feet and jumped into the dark hole. "Guys, we're going to eat like kings!" They didn't respond. When his eyes adjusted to the dark, he realized they were slumped over. "Hey, wake up! Food!"

He shook them gently, then harder. And then he knew. And then he cried.

For the next three weeks, Choon plodded in the snow, wind, and cold, thinking only about one thing: *America, America, America.* That sole thought kept him going on days when he couldn't find food, when he wanted to give up. Finally, the gutsy boy reached a Marine base where he stayed until the end of the war in 1953. "I don't want to be a spy anymore," he told the soldiers. "I want to be an American."

Choon remained with the 1st Marines, working as a translator in Seoul. In 1955, when he was 18, three Marines who had befriended him, paid his way to come to the United States and live out his dream. Choon eventually became an American citizen and changed his name to Eddie Ko. He married and had two children, whom he named after the two fallen GIs, Al and Harry. Since 1991, he and his wife, Joanna, have owned the Quail Hollow Golf and Country Club in Wesley Chapel, Florida.

About the
Author

Allan Zullo is the author of nearly 90 nonfiction books on subjects ranging from sports and the supernatural to history and animals.

He has written the best-selling Haunted Kids series, published by Scholastic, which are filled with chilling stories based on, or inspired by, documented cases from the files of ghost hunters. Allan also has introduced Scholastic readers to the Ten True Tales series, about kids who have met the challenges of dangerous, sometimes life-threatening, situations. In addition, he has authored two books about the real-life experiences of kids during the Holocaust—*Survivors: True Stories of Children in the Holocaust* and *Heroes of the Holocaust: True Stories of Rescues by Teens*.

Allan, the grandfather of two boys and the father of two grown daughters, lives with his wife Kathryn on the side of a mountain near Asheville, North Carolina. To learn more about the author, visit his Web site at www.allanzullo.com.